PETERSON CASCONE O'CONNOR VACHUSKA DAVIE

Software-Defined Networks

A Systems Approach

SYSTEMS APPROACH LLC

Contents

Foreword

I got goosebumps when I saw the first Mosaic web browser in 1993. Something big was clearly about to happen; I had no idea how big. The Internet immediately exploded in scale, with thousands of new ISPs (Internet Service Providers) popping up everywhere, each grafting on a new piece of the Internet. All they needed to do was plug interoperable pieces together—off-the-shelf commercial switches, routers, base-stations, and access points sold by traditional networking equipment vendors—with no need to ask permission from a central controlling authority. The early routers were simple and streamlined—they just needed to support the Internet protocol. Decentralized control let the Internet grow rapidly.

The router manufacturers faced a dilemma: It's hard to maintain a thriving profitable business selling devices that are simple and streamlined. What's more, if a big network of simple devices is easy to manage remotely, all the intelligence (and value) is provided by the network operator, not the router manufacturer. So the external API was kept minimal ("network management" was considered a joke) and the routers were jam-packed with new features to keep all the value inside. By the mid 2000s, routers used by ISPs were so complicated that they supported hundreds of protocols and were based on more than 100 million lines of source code – ironically, more than ten times the complexity of the largest telephone exchange ever built. The Internet paid a hefty price for this complexity: routers were bloated, power hungry, unreliable, hard to secure, and crazy expensive. Worst of all, they were hard to improve (ISPs needed to beg equipment vendors to add new capabilities) and it was impossible for an ISP to add their own new features. Network owners complained of a "stranglehold" by the router vendors, and the research community warned that the Internet was "ossified."

This book is the story of what happened next, and it's an exciting one. Larry, Carmelo, Brian, Thomas and Bruce capture clearly, through concrete examples and open-source code: How those who own and operate big networks started to write their own code and build their own switches and routers. Some chose to replace routers with homegrown devices that were simpler and easier to maintain; others chose to move the software off the router to a remote, centralized control plane. Whichever path they chose, open-source became a bigger and bigger part. Once open-source had proved itself in Linux, Apache, Mozilla and Kubernetes, it was ready to be trusted to run our networks too.

This book explains why the SDN movement happened. It was essentially about a change in control: the owners and operators of big networks took control of how their networks work, grabbing the keys to innovation from the equipment vendors. It started with data center companies because they couldn't build big-enough scale-out networks using off-the-shelf networking equipment. So they bought switching chips and wrote the software themselves. Yes, it saved them money (often reducing the cost by a factor of five or more), but it was control they were after. They employed armies of software engineers to ignite a Cambrian explosion of new ideas in networking, making their networks more reliable, quicker to fix, and with better control over their traffic. Today, in 2021, all of the large data center companies build their own networking equipment: they download and modify open-source control software, or they write or commission software to control their networks. They have taken control. The ISPs and 5G operators are next. Within a decade, expect enterprise and campus networks to run on open-source control software, managed from the cloud. This is a good change, because only those who own and operate networks at scale know how to do it best.

This change—a revolution in how networks are built, towards homegrown software developed and maintained by the network operator—is called Software Defined Networking (SDN). The authors have been part of this revolution since the very beginning, and have captured how and why it came about.

They also help us see what future networks will be like. Rather than being built by plugging together a bunch of boxes running standardized interoperability protocols, a network system will be a platform we can program ourselves. The network owner will decide how the network works by programming whatever behavior they wish. Students of networking will learn how to programme a distributed system, rather than study the arcane details of legacy protocols.

For anyone interested in programming, networks just got interesting again. And this book is an excellent place to start.

Nick McKeown
Stanford, California

Preface

The Internet is the midst of a transformation, one that moves away from bundled proprietary devices, and instead embraces disaggregating network hardware (which becomes commodity) from the software that controls it (which scales in the cloud). The transformation is generally known as *Software-Defined Networking (SDN),* but because it is disrupting the marketplace, it is challenging to untangle business positioning from technical fundamentals, from short-term engineering decisions. This book provides such an untangling, where the most important thing we hope readers take away is an understanding of an SDN-based network as a scalable distributed system running on commodity hardware.

Anyone who has taken an introductory networking class recognizes the protocol stack as the canonical framework for describing the network. Whether that stack has seven layers or just three, it shapes and constrains the way we think about computer networks. Textbooks are organized accordingly. SDN suggests an alternative world-view, one that comes with a new software stack. This book is organized around that new stack, with the goal of presenting a top-to-bottom tour of SDN without leaving any significant gaps that the reader might suspect can only be filled with magic or proprietary code. *We invite you do the hands-on programming exercises included at the end of the book to prove to yourself that the software stack is both real and complete.*

An important aspect of meeting this goal is to use open source. We do this in large part by taking advantage of two community-based organizations that are leading the way. One is the *Open Compute Project (OCP),* which is actively specifying and certifying commodity hardware (e.g., bare-metal switches) upon which the SDN software stack runs. The second is the *Open Networking Foundation (ONF)*, which is actively implementing a suite of software components that can be integrated into an end-to-end solution. There are many other players in this space—from incumbent vendors to network operators, startups, standards bodies, and other open source projects—each offering varied interpretations of what SDN *is* and *is not*. We discuss these other perspectives and explain how they fit into the larger scheme of things, but we do not let them deter us from describing the full breadth of SDN. Only time will tell where the SDN journey takes us, but we believe it is important to understand the scope of the opportunity.

This book assumes a general understanding of the Internet, although a deeper appreciation for the role switches and routers play forwarding ethernet frames and IP packets is helpful. Links to related background information are included to help bridge any gaps. This book is also a work-in-progress. We are eager to hear your feedback and suggestions.

Acknowledgements

The software described in this book is due to the hard work of the ONF engineering team and the open source community that works with them. We acknowledge their contributions, with a special thank-you to Yi Tseng, Max Pudelko, and Charles Chan for their contributions to the tutorials that this book includes as hands-on exercises. We also thank Charles Chan, Jennifer Rexford, and Nick McKeown for their feedback on early drafts of the manuscript.

Larry Peterson, Carmelo Cascone, Brian O'Connor, Thomas Vachuska,
   and Bruce Davie
December 2020

Chapter 1: Introduction

Software-Defined Networking (SDN) is an approach to how we *implement* networks, which matters because it impacts the *pace of innovation*. SDN does not directly address any of the technical challenges of routing, congestion control, traffic engineering, security, mobility, reliability, or real-time communication, but it does open new opportunities to create and deploy innovative solutions to these and similar problems. Exactly how SDN accomplishes this has both business and technical implications, which we discuss throughout this book.

Our approach is to view SDN through a *systems lens*, which is to say, we explore the collection of design principles that guide the journey to realizing software-defined networks (a journey that is still in progress), rather than to talk about SDN as though it were a point solution. Our approach emphasizes concepts (bringing abstractions to networking is a key part of the original case for SDN), but to keep the discussion concrete, we also draw on our experience implementing a collection of open source platforms over the last six years. These platforms are being used to deliver SDN-based solutions into production networks, including Tier-1 network operators.

This focus on the software stack is a central theme of the book. Because SDN is an approach to building networks, a set of software and hardware artifacts is required to put that approach into practice. The open source examples we draw upon are available on GitHub, with links to both code and hands-on programming exercises available throughout the book.

Before getting into the details, it is helpful to understand the origin story for SDN, which started as an effort by the Computer Science research community to address the ossification of the Internet, opening it up to more rapid innovation. That history is well-documented in an article by Feamster, Rexford, and Zegura.

We add two footnotes to that history. The first is a 2001 National Academy report, which brought the ossification of the Internet into focus as a major challenge. In doing so, the report catalyzed what turned out to be a 20-year R&D effort. The fruits of that research are now directly impacting networks being deployed by Cloud Providers, enterprises, and Internet Service Providers.

The second is Scott Shenker's iconic presentation making the intellectual case for SDN. Understanding the central thesis of Shenker's talk—that the practice of building and operating networks is in dire need of abstractions to help manage complexity—is the linchpin to also understanding the systems, platforms, tools, and interfaces described in this book.

1.1 Market Landscape

To fully appreciate the role and ultimate impact of SDN, it is important to start by looking at the market landscape. SDN was in part conceived as a way to transform the marketplace, inspired by the transformation that the computing industry went through in previous decades.

The computing industry was historically structured as a *vertical market*. This meant that a customer wanting a solution to some problem (e.g., finance, design, analysis) bought a vertically integrated solution from a single vendor, typically a large mainframe company like IBM. The vertically integrated solution included everything from the underlying hardware (including processor chips), to the operating system running on that hardware, to the application itself.

As shown in Figure 1, the introduction of microprocessors (e.g., Intel x86 and Motorola 68000) and open source OS's (e.g., BSD Unix and Linux), helped transform that vertical market into a horizontal marketplace, with open interfaces spurring innovation at every level.

Further Reading:
N. Feamster, J. Rexford, and E. Zegura. The Road to SDN: An Intellectual History of Programmable Networks. SIGCOMM CCR, April 2014.

Further Reading:
Looking Over the Fence at Networks: A Neighbor's View of Networking Research. The National Academies Press, 2001.

Further Reading:
S. Shenker. The Future of Networking and the Past of Protocols. Open Networking Summit, October 2011.

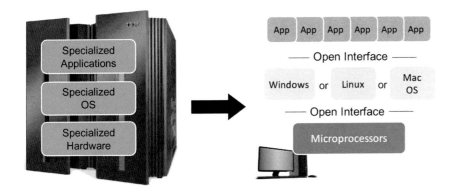

Figure 1: Transformation of the vertical mainframe market to a horizontal marketplace with open interfaces and multiple options available at every level.

SDN, when viewed as a transformative initiative, is an attempt to spur the same sort of changes in the networking industry, which as the 2001 National Academy report observed, had ossified. As shown in Figure 2, the end goal is a horizontal ecosystem with multiple network operating systems enabled on top of bare-metal switches[1] built from merchant silicon switching chips, which in turn enable a rich marketplace of networking applications.

[1] The term "bare-metal" originated in the server world to refer to a machine without either an OS or hypervisor installed. By analogy, the term has come to apply to switches provided without a bundled operating system or set of networking applications. Disaggregating the switching hardware from the software is central to SDN.

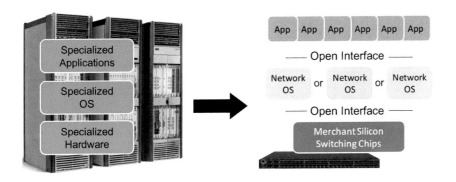

Figure 2: Transformation of the vertical router market to a horizontal marketplace with open interfaces and multiple options available at every level.

The value of such a transformation is clear. Opening a vertically integrated, closed, and proprietary market creates opportunities for innovation that would not otherwise be available. Or to put it another way: by opening up these interfaces, it becomes possible to shift control from the vendors that sell networking equipment to the network operators that build networks to meet their users' needs.

To understand this opportunity in more depth, we need to get into the technical details (which we introduce in the next section), but appreciating the backstory of SDN as a means to transform the networking industry is an important place to start.

1.2 Technical Landscape

With the understanding that SDN is an approach rather than a point solution, it is helpful to define the design principles at the core of that approach. Framing the design space is the goal of this section, but one important takeaway is that there is more than one possible end-state. Each network operator is free to pick different design points, and build out their network accordingly.

That said, this book makes a point of describing the most complete application of SDN principles, which is sometimes called *pure play SDN*. Given that the whole point of SDN is to disrupt the existing vertical market, it should come as no surprise that incumbent vendors would offer *hybrid* solutions that align with their established business models and ease adoption. We sometimes call these hybrid solutions *SDN-lite* because they take advantage of some aspects of SDN, but not the full spectrum. Apart from pointing out the existence of these partial solutions, we do not attempt to be encyclopedic in our coverage of them. Our goal is to chart the full potential of SDN, and do so with as much technical depth as today's state-of-the-art allows.

1.2.1 Disaggregating the Control and Data Planes

The seminal idea behind SDN is that networks have distinct *control* and *data* planes, and the separation of these two planes should be codified in an open interface. In the most basic terms, the control plane determines *how* the network should behave, while the data plane is responsible for implementing that behavior on individual packets. For example, one job of the control plane is to determine the route packets should follow through the network (perhaps by running a routing protocol like BGP, OSPF, or RIP), and the task of forwarding packets along those routes is the job of the data plane, in which switches making forwarding decisions at each hop on a packet-by-packet basis.

In practice, decoupling the control and data planes manifests in parallel but distinct data structures: the control plane maintains a *routing table* that includes any auxiliary information needed to select the best route at a given point in time (e.g., including alternative paths, their respective costs, and any policy constraints), while the data plane maintains a *forwarding table* that is optimized for fast packet processing (e.g., determining that any packet arriving on Port i with destination address D should be transmitted out Port j, optionally with a new destination address D'). The routing table is often called the *Routing Information Base (RIB)* and the forwarding table is often called the *Forwarding Information Base (FIB)*, as depicted in Figure 3.

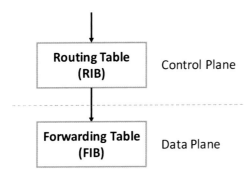

Figure 3: Control plane (and corresponding RIB) decoupled from the data plane (and the corresponding FIB).

There is no controversy about the value of decoupling the network control and data planes. It is a well-established practice in networking, where closed/proprietary routers that pre-date SDN adopted this level of modularity. But the first principle of SDN is that the interface between the control and data planes should be both well-defined and open. This strong level of modularity is often referred to as *disaggregation*, and it makes it possible for different parties to be responsible for each plane.

In principle then, disaggregation means that a network operator should be able to purchase their control plane from vendor X and their data plane from vendor Y. Although it did not happen immediately, one natural consequence of disaggregation is that the data plane components (i.e., the switches) become commodity packet forwarding devices—commonly referred to as *bare-metal switches*—with all the intelligence implemented in software and running in the control plane.[2] This is exactly what happened in the computer industry, where microprocessors became commodity. Chapter 4 describes these bare-metal switches in more detail.

[2] By our count, over 15 open-source and proprietary disaggregated control planes are available today.

Disaggregating the control and data planes implies the need for a well-defined *forwarding abstraction*, that is, a general-purpose way for the control plane to instruct the data plane to forward packets in a particular way. Keeping in mind disaggregation should **not** restrict how a given switch vendor implements the data plane (e.g., the exact form of its forwarding table or the process by which it forwards packets), this forwarding abstraction should not assume (or favor) one data plane implementation over another.

The original interface supporting disaggregation, called *OpenFlow*, was introduced in 2008,[3] and although it was hugely instrumental in launching the SDN journey, it proved to be only a small part of what defines SDN today. Equating SDN with OpenFlow significantly under-values SDN, but it is an important milestone because it introduced *Flow Rules* as a simple-but-powerful way to specify the forwarding behavior.

[3] OpenFlow was actually not the first effort to do this; it was the one that got the most traction. Earlier efforts included Ipsilon's GSMP and the ForCES work at the IETF.

A flow rule is a Match-Action pair: Any packet that *Matches* the first part of the rule should have the associated *Action* applied to it. A simple flow rule, for example, might specify that any packet with destination address D be forwarded on output port i. The original OpenFlow spec allowed the header fields shown in Figure 4 to be included in the Match half of the rule. So for example, a Match might specify a packet's MAC header Type field equals 0x800 (indicating the frame carries and IP packet) and its IP header DstAddr field be contained in some subnet (e.g., 192.12.69/24).

The Actions originally included *"forward packet to one or more ports"* and *"drop packet,"* plus a *"send packet up to the control plane"* escape hatch for any packet that requires further processing by a *controller* (a term introduced to signify the process running in the control plane responsible for controlling the switch). The set of allowed Actions became more complex over time, which we will return to later.

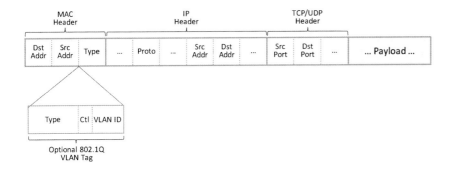

Figure 4: Header Fields Matched in Original OpenFlow Specification.

Building on the flow rule abstraction, each switch then maintains a *Flow Table* to store the set of flow rules the controller has passed to it. In effect, the flow table is the OpenFlow abstraction for the forwarding table introduced at the beginning of this section. OpenFlow also defined a secure protocol with which flow rules could be passed between the controller and the switch, making it possible to run the controller off-switch. This enabled the configuration shown in Figure 5.

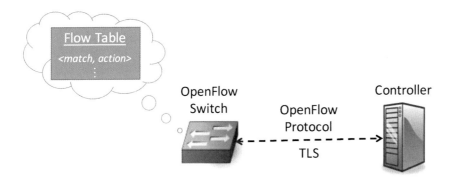

Figure 5: Controller securely passes flow rules to an OpenFlow-enabled switch, which maintains a Flow Table.

OpenFlow grew more complicated over time (and was certainly defined with much more precision than the previous paragraphs), but the original idea was purposely simple. At the time (2008), the idea of building a switch that included an "OpenFlow option" in addition to its conventional forwarding path was a radical idea, proposed under the pretense of enabling research. In fact, the original OpenFlow publication was written as a call-to-action to the research community.

Further Reading:
N. McKeown, et. al. OpenFlow: Enabling Innovation in Campus Networks. SIGCOMM CCR, March 2008.

Today, the OpenFlow specification has been through multiple revisions, and work is underway to replace it with a more flexible (i.e., programmable) alternative. We return to OpenFlow—and P4, the alternative programming language—in Chapter 4.

We conclude this section by calling attention to two related but distinct concepts: *Control* and *Configuration*. The idea of OpenFlow (and SDN in general) is to define an interface for controlling the data plane, which implies making real-time decisions about how to respond to link and switch failures, as well as other data plane events. If the data plane reports a failure, the control plane needs to learn about this failure and provide a remedy (e.g., a new Match/Action flow rule) generally within milliseconds.[4] Otherwise, the disaggregation implied by SDN would not be viable.

At the same time, operators are accustomed to configuring their switches and routers. This has historically been done using a *Command Line Interface (CLI)* or (less commonly) a management protocol like SNMP. Looking back at Figure 3, this corresponds to the northbound interface to the RIB (as opposed to the interface between the RIB and the FIB). This interface is capable of installing new routes, which on the surface seems to be equivalent to installing a new flow rule. Would a switch be considered "SDN-capable" if it merely exposed a programmatic configuration interface in lieu of the CLI?

The answer is likely no, and it comes down to hitting the mark on both generality and performance. While a well-defined programmatic configuration interface is certainly an improvement over legacy CLIs, they are intended for modifying various settings of the control plane (such as RIB entries) and other device parameters (e.g., port speeds/modes) rather than modifying the data plane's FIB. As a consequence, such configuration interfaces are (a) unlikely to support the full range of programmability implied by a control/data plane interface, and (b) unlikely to support the real-time control loop required by control/data plane disaggregation. In short, the momentum of SDN has had the side-effect of improving the configuration interfaces exposed by switch and router vendors (and we describe the state-of-the-art in such interfaces in Chapter 5), but doing so is not a substitute for the granularity of control SDN requires.

[4] There are also events that require attention in sub-millisecond response times. In such cases it is necessary to implement the remedy in the data plane, and then inform the control plane, giving it the opportunity to re-program the data plane. Fast failover groups are an example of this in OpenFlow.

To be clear, all elements in a switch require configuration. The data plane requires configuration of things like port speeds. The platform requires configuration of fans, LEDs, and other peripherals. The on-switch software needs to be informed what certificate it should use when a client connects and what log level should be set. The control plane components also require configuration. For example, the routing agent needs to know its IP address, who its neighbors are, and if it has any static routes. The key distinction is the purpose, but more quantitatively, the rate of updates: configuration implies potentially thousands of updates/day while control implies potentially thousands of updates/sec.

1.2.2 Control Plane: Centralized vs Distributed

Having disaggregated the control and data planes, the next consideration is how to implement the control plane. One option is to run the software that implements the control plane *on-switch*. Doing so implies each switch operates as an autonomous device, communicating with its peer switches throughout the network to construct a local routing table. Conveniently, there already exists a set of protocols that can be used for this purpose: BGP, OSPF, RIP, and so on. This is exactly the *distributed control plane* the Internet has employed for the last 30+ years.

There is value in this scenario. Because disaggregation led to the availability of low-cost bare-metal switches built using merchant silicon switching chips, network operators can buy hardware from bare-metal switching vendors, and then load the appropriate control plane software from some other vendor, or possibly even use an open source version of those protocols. Doing so potentially lowers costs and reduces complexity (because only the required control modules need to be loaded onto the device), but it does not necessarily realize the pace of innovation SDN promises. This is because the operator remains stuck in the slow-paced standardization processes implied by today's standardized protocols. It also fails to deliver the new networking abstractions envisioned by SDN's pioneers (as in Shenker's talk noted above, for example).

The alternative, which is the second design principle of SDN, is that the control plane should be fully independent of the data plane and logically centralized. This implies the control plane is implemented *off-switch*, for example, by running the controller in the cloud.[5]

We say logically centralized because while the state collected by the controller is maintained in a global data structure (think of this as the centralized counterpart to the per-switch routing table), the implementation of this data structure could still be distributed over multiple servers, as is now the best practice for cloud-hosted, horizontally scalable services. This is important for both scalability and availability, where the key is that the two planes are configured and scaled independent of each other. If you need more capacity in the data plane you add a bare-metal switch. If you need more capacity in the control plane you add a compute server (or more likely, a virtual machine).

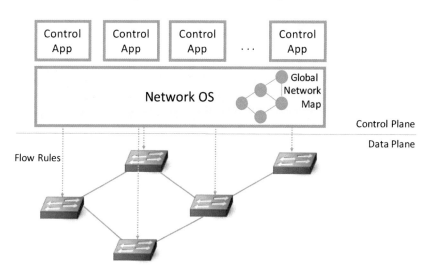

Figure 6 depicts the centralized control plane associated with a distributed data plane, but goes a step further by also introducing one of the key components implied by this approach: a *Network Operating System (NOS)*. Like a server operating system (e.g., Linux, iOS, Android, Windows) that provides a set of high-level abstractions that make it easier to implement applications (e.g., users can read and write files instead of directly accessing disk drives), a NOS makes it

[5] For completeness, we note that it is also possible to adopt a mixed approach, with some control functionality running on-switch and some running off-switch, in a cloud-hosted controller.

Figure 6: Network Operating System (NOS) hosting a set of control applications and providing a logically centralized point of control for an underlying network data plane.

easier to implement network control functionality, otherwise known as *Control Apps*.

The idea behind the NOS is to abstract the details of the switches and provide a *Network Map* abstraction to the application developer. The NOS detects changes in the underlying network (e.g., switches, ports, and links going up-and-down) and the control application simply implements the behavior it wants on this abstract graph. This means the NOS takes on the burden of collecting network state (the hard part of distributed algorithms like Link-State and Distance-Vector routing protocols) and the app is free to simply run the shortest path algorithm on this graph and load the resulting flow rules into the underlying switches. An introduction to Link-State and Distance-Vector routing algorithms is available online.

By centralizing this logic, it becomes possible to do something that wasn't previously possible in distributed networks: compute globally optimized solutions. As we discuss in later chapters, the published evidence from cloud providers that have embraced this approach confirms this advantage. It was well understood for many years that the fully distributed approach of the Internet did not lend itself to global optimizations, but until SDN, there wasn't really a feasible alternative. SDN brings this possibility to fruition. This is the power of offering a centralized network abstraction.

The idea of "collecting network state" is central to SDN and the role played by a NOS. We are not talking about collecting the full range of network telemetry data that is used to troubleshoot misconfigurations or do long-term planning, but we are talking about fine-grain meters that may require an immediate control plane response, an obvious example being the number of bytes/packets sent and received on each port. Protocols like OpenFlow define the means to report such meters to the NOS, in addition to providing the means for the NOS to install new flow rules based on the information it collects.

There is a related benefit of control plane centralization that will become clearer as we get into SDN use cases. A logically centralized control plane provides a single point to expose network APIs. The idea of putting programmatic APIs on individual switches and routers has been around for decades, but failed to make much impact. By

Further Reading:
Routing. *Computer Networks: A Systems Approach*, 2020.

contrast, a central API to an entire collection of switches or routers has enabled all sorts of new use cases. These include network virtualization, network automation, and network verification. To take the example of automation, it's quite hard to automate something like BGP configuration because it so hard to reason about how a set of BGP speakers will respond when they all start talking to each other. But if your central control plane exposes an API in which you can say "create an isolated network that connects the following set of endpoints" then it is quite reasonable to make that request part of an automated configuration system. This is precisely what happens in many modern clouds, where the provisioning of network resources and policies is automated along with all sort of other operations such as spinning up virtual machines or containers.

Domain of Control

The "Centralized vs Decentralized" framing of this section is intended to characterize one dimension of the SDN design space, not to indicate that network operators face an either-or situation. There are many factors that impact where a given operator comes down on this spectrum, but one place to start is to scope the domain to which SDN is being applied. We discuss example use cases in Chapter 2, but there is a natural evolution of networking that highlights the thought process.

Historically, there has been one control plane instance per switch and they both run together on the same box. As simple routers grew into chassis routers, there were typically N control plane instances for M line cards. They ran on discrete hardware and talked to each other through a management network. As chassis routers grew into a multi-rack fabric built from commodity switches, SDN suggested a design that aggregates forwarding elements under a control plane running anywhere and structured as a distributed system. The advantage is that such a system can use modern techniques for state distribution and management, rather than being tied to standards. The key is to find domains for which it is possible to optimize performance with a logically centralized control plane.

Returning to the original question of centralized versus distributed control plane, proponents of the latter often base their rationale on the historical reasons the Internet adopted distributed routing protocols in the first place: scale, and survival in the face of failures. The concern is that any centralized solution results in a bottleneck that is also a single point-of-failure. Distributing the centralized control plane over a cluster of servers mitigates both these concerns, as techniques developed in the distributed systems world can ensure both high availability and scalability of such clusters.

A secondary concern raised about control plan centralization is that, since the control plane is remote (i.e., off-switch), the link between the two planes adds a vulnerable attack surface. The counter-argument is that non-SDN networks already have (and depend on) out-of-band management networks, so this attack surface is not a new one. These management networks can be used by off-switch controllers just as readily as by other management software. There is also the argument that a small number of centralized controllers can present a smaller attack surface than a large number of distributed controllers. Suffice it to say, opinions differ, but there is certainly a wealth of support for the centralized approach.

1.2.3 Data Plane: Programmable vs Fixed-Function

The final dimension of the design space is whether the switches that implement the data plane are programmable or fixed-function. To appreciate what this means, we need to say a little more about how switches are implemented.

The preceding discussion has implied a simple model of a switch, in which the switch's main processing loop receives a packet from an input port, does a lookup of the destination address in the FIB (or using OpenFlow terminology, in the flow table), and puts the packet on the output port or port group indicated by the matched table entry. This is a reasonable implementation strategy for low-end switches (i.e., the main processing loop is implemented in software on a general-purpose processor), but high-performance switches employ a hardware-based *forwarding pipeline*.

We postpone an in-depth description of these pipelines until Chapter 4, but the important characteristic for now is whether that pipeline is limited to matching a fixed set of fields in the packet headers (e.g., the fields shown in Figure 4) and perform a fixed set of actions, or if the bit-patterns to be matched and the actions to be executed are dynamically programmed into the switch. The former are referred to as *fixed-function pipelines* and the latter as *programmable pipelines*. But first we have to answer the question: "What exactly is a forwarding pipeline?"

One way to think about a forwarding pipeline is that instead of a single flow table, as suggested in the previous section, switches actually implement a series of flow tables, each focused on a subset of the header fields that might be involved in a given flow rule (e.g., one table matches the MAC header, one matches the IP header, and so on). A given packet is processed by multiple flow tables in sequence—i.e., a pipeline—to determine how it is ultimately forwarded. Figure 7 gives a generic schematic for such a pipeline of flow tables, based on a diagram in the OpenFlow specification. The idea is that a set of actions are accumulated as the packet flows through the pipeline, and executed as a set in the last stage.

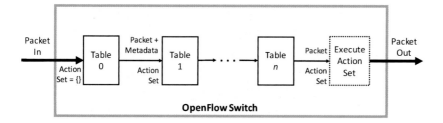

Figure 7: Simple Schematic of an OpenFlow Forwarding Pipeline.

At first glance this might not seem to be important since header fields like those shown in Figure 4 are both well-known and at easy-to-compute offsets in every packet a switch has to forward (e.g., Table 0 tries to match the MAC header fields, Table 1 tries to match the IP fields, and so on). And to this point, the initial idea of SDN was purposely data plane agnostic—SDN was entirely focused on opening the control plane to programmability. But early experience implementing SDN controllers exposed two problems.

The first problem was that as SDN matured from a research experiment to a viable alternative to legacy, proprietary switches, performance became increasingly important. And while flow rules were general enough to say what forwarding behavior the controller wanted to program into a switch, switches didn't necessarily have the capacity to implement that functionality in an efficient way. To ensure high forwarding performance, flow tables were implemented using highly optimized data structures that required specialized memories, like *Ternary Content Addressable Memory (TCAM)*. As a consequence, they supported only a limited number of entries, which meant the controller had to be careful about how they were used.

In short, it proved necessary for the controller to know details about the pipeline in order to install a set of flow rules that the switch could map to hardware. As a consequence, many control applications were implicitly tied to a particular forwarding pipeline. This would be analogous to writing a Java or Python program that can only run on an x86 processor and is not easily ported to an ARM processor. It proved necessary to have more control over the forwarding pipeline, and because we don't want to limit ourselves to a single vendor's pipeline, we also need an abstract way to specify a pipeline's behavior, that can in turn be mapped onto the physical pipeline of any given switch.

The second problem was that the protocol stack changed in unexpected ways, meaning that the assumption that all header fields you might need to match against are well-known is flawed. For example, while OpenFlow (and early forwarding pipelines) correctly include support for VLAN tags, a cornerstone for creating virtual networks in enterprise networks, the 4096 possible VLANs was not sufficient to account for all the tenants that a cloud might host.

To address this problem, the IETF introduced a new encapsulation, called *Virtual Extensible LAN (VXLAN)*. Unlike the original approach, which encapsulated a virtualized ethernet frame inside another ethernet frame, VXLAN encapsulates a virtual ethernet frame inside a UDP packet. Figure 8 shows the VXLAN header, along with all the packet headers a switch might have to process to make a forwarding decision.

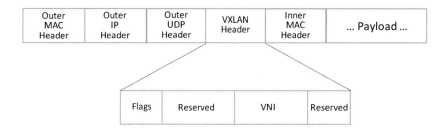

Figure 8: VXLAN Header encapsulated in a UDP/IP packet.

Adding support for VXLAN to OpenFlow is hard enough since agreeing to standards takes time, but adding support for VXLAN to fixed-function forwarding pipelines is an even more time-consuming endeavor: *Hardware needs to change!* One could argue that with VXLAN we are now done changing the protocol stack, but that's unlikely. For example, QUIC is gaining momentum as an alternative to TCP when used with HTTP. Another example on the horizon is MPLS vs SRv6. Even VXLAN is now being superseded in some settings by a new, more flexible encapsulation called GENEVE.

Programmable forwarding pipelines, coupled with a high-level language that can be used to program the pipeline, is one viable response to these two issues. Both have emerged in the last few years, in the form of a *Protocol Independent Switching Architecture (PISA)* and the *P4* programming language. We will discuss both in more detail in Chapter 4, but the big takeaway for now is that SDN has evolved beyond its original goal as a means to program the control plane. Today, SDN also includes the possibility of a programmable data plane.

1.3 SDN: A Definition

To summarize, the original definition of SDN is simple to state:

> *A network in which the control plane is physically separate from the forwarding plane, and a single control plane controls several forwarding devices.*[6]

[6] From Nick McKeown's 2013 presentation entitled *Software Defined Networking*.

This is a succinct way of saying what Sections 1.2.1 and 1.2.2 explain in long-form. Since that original definition, SDN has been interpreted by different stakeholders to mean both *less* (e.g., a programmatic configuration interface to network devices qualifies as SDN) and *more* (e.g., SDN also includes switches with programmable forwarding pipelines). This book covers the full spectrum by taking the more expansive view.

Another way to frame SDN is to think of it as having two phases. In Phase 1, network operators took ownership of the control plane, and now in Phase 2, they are taking control of how packets are processed in the data plane. Phase 2 is still a work-in-progress, but as Nick McKeown posits, the aspirational end state is one in which:

> *"Networks will [hopefully] be programmed by many, and operated by few."*

Which is to say, SDN is not just about shifting control from vendors to operators, but ultimately, it is about shifting control from vendors to operators to users. That's the long-term goal, inspired by what commodity servers and open source software did for the computing industry. But we still have a ways to go, so we return to more modest predictions about the next phase of the SDN journey in Chapter 8.

Further Reading:
N. McKeown. FutureNet 2019. October 2019.

Chapter 2: Use Cases

A good way to understand the value of SDN is to look at how it is used in practice. Doing so also helps explain the different perspectives on what SDN means, corresponding to what we refer to as "pure play" versus "hybrid/lite" Software-Defined Networking in the previous chapter. But before getting into *how* SDN is used, we start by first summarizing *who* is using it.

First, SDN has been embraced and widely deployed by cloud providers, with Google, Facebook, and Microsoft being the most public about adoption. While their platforms and solutions are still mostly proprietary, they have open sourced individual components in an effort to catalyze wider adoption. We discuss these individual components in later chapters.

Second, large network operators like AT&T, DT, NTT, and Comcast publicly talk about their plans to deploy SDN-based solutions—especially in their access networks—but they are proceeding cautiously, with most of their initiatives either using hybrid approaches, or in the case of pure play SDN, still in the trial phase. The most notable exception is Comcast, which has deployed the open source components described in this book throughout their production network.

Finally, enterprises have begun to adopt SDN, but there are two things to note about this situation. One is that while pure play SDN is deployed in some Universities, with the goal of supporting research and innovation, adoption is slower for enterprises in general. The most likely path-to-adoption for pure play SDN by enterprises is via managed edge services offered by cloud providers. The idea is to connect on-premise clusters running edge workloads with public clouds running scalable datacenter workloads. The second is that many enterprise vendors offer SDN products, where the focus has been more on the benefits of logical control plane centralization rather than open interfaces to the data plane. Network virtualization and SD-WAN (software-defined wide area networks) have both had considerable success in the enterprise, as discussed below.

2.1 Network Virtualization

The first widely-adopted use case for SDN was to virtualize the network. Virtual networks, including both *Virtual Private Networks (VPNs)* and *Virtual Local Area Networks (VLANs)*, have been a part of the Internet for years. VLANs have historically proven useful within enterprises, where they are used to isolate different organizational groups, such as departments or labs, giving each of them the appearance of having their own private LAN. However, these early forms of virtualization were quite limited in scope and lacked many of the advantages of SDN. You could think of them as virtualizing the address space of a network but not all its other properties, such as firewall policies or higher-level network services like load balancing.

The original idea behind using SDN to create virtual networks is widely credited to the team at Nicira, whose approach is described in in an NSDI paper by Teemu Koponen and colleagues. The key insight was that modern clouds required networks that could be programmatically created, managed, and torn down, without a sysadmin having to manually configure, say, VLAN tags on some number of network switches. By separating the control plane from the data plane, and logically centralizing the control plane, it became possible to expose a single API entry point for the creation, modification, and deletion of virtual networks. This meant that the same automation systems that were being used to provision compute and storage capacity in a cloud (such as OpenStack at the time) could now programmatically provision a virtual network with appropriate policies to interconnect those other resources.

The rise of network virtualization followed by several years the rise of compute virtualization, and was very much enabled by it. Compute

Further Reading:
T. Koponen et al. Network Virtualization in Multi-tenant Datacenters. NSDI, April, 2014.

virtualization made manual server provisioning a thing of the past, and exposed the manual and time-consuming processes of network configuration as the "long pole" in delivering a cloud service. Virtual machine migration, which enabled running VMs to move from one network location to another (taking their IP addresses with them), further exposed the limitations of manual network configuration. This need to automate network provisioning was first recognized by large cloud providers but eventually became mainstream in enterprises.

As microservices and container-based systems such as Kubernetes have gained in popularity, network virtualization has continued to evolve to meet the needs of these environments. There are a range of open source network "plugins" (Calico, Flannel, Antrea, etc.) that provide network virtualization services for Kubernetes.

Because network virtualization set out to deliver a full set of network services in a programmatic way, its impact went beyond the simplification and automation of network provisioning. As virtual networks became lightweight objects, created and destroyed as needed, with a full set of services (such as stateful firewalling, deep-packet inspection, and so on), a new approach to network security was enabled. Rather than adding security features after the network was created, security features could be created as an inherent part of the network itself. Furthermore, with no limit on how many virtual networks could be created, as approach known as *microsegmentation* took hold. This entails the creation of fine-grained, isolated networks (microsegments) specific to the needs of, say, a group of processes implementing a single distributed application. Microsegmentation offers clear benefits over prior approaches to network security, dramatically reducing the attack surface and the impact of attacks spreading throughout an enterprise or data center.

Bringing SDN to Life

As we saw in Chapter 1, the ideas behind SDN had been in the works for years, but there were two related events that, looking back, had a significant impact in bringing the concept of programmable networks from theory to practice. First was the 2007 founding of the commercial startup Nicira Networks. Nicira was founded by three of the acknowledged pioneers of SDN: Martin Casado, Scott Shenker, and Nick McKeown. While Nicira was founded to make commercial use of SDN, as with many startups, it took a while to find the ideal product for the marketplace. In the end, it was Network Virtualization that became the industry's first successful application of SDN. Nicira's network virtualization platform first shipped in 2011, establishing the category and ultimately paving the way for VMware's acquisition of the company and subsequent development of VMware NSX.

At around the same time, McKeown and Shenker also created three non-profit organizations to catalyze the SDN transformation across the networking industry: the Open Networking Foundation (ONF) took on responsibility for advancing the cause of network disaggregation, including development of the OpenFlow standard; the Open Networking Laboratory (ON.Lab) was created to produce open source SDN-based solutions and platforms; and the Open Networking Summit (ONS) was created as a conference platform to bring together academics and practitioners interested in SDN. In 2018, ONF and ON.Lab merged, and the combined organization has focused on building the open source software that is highlighted throughout this book.

Of course there have been many other startups, conferences, and consortia that have driven the development of SDN to where it is today, and the effects of their work can be seen throughout this chapter.

It's worth noting that to create virtual networks as we have described, it is necessary to encapsulate packets from the virtual networks in a way that lets them traverse the underlying physical network. As a simple example, a virtual network can have its own private address space which is decoupled from the underlying physical address space. For this reason, virtual networks have used a range of encapsulation techniques, of which VXLAN (briefly discussed in Chapter 1) is probably the most well known. In recent years, a more flexible encapsulation called GENEVE (Generic Network Virtualization Encapsulation) has emerged.

There have been reasonable debates about whether network virtualization is really SDN. Certainly it displays many of the properties we discussed in the previous chapter—the original Nicira network virtualization platform even used OpenFlow to communicate between its central controller and the data plane elements. And the centralization benefits of SDN are at the core of what made network virtualization possible, particularly as an enabler of network automation. On the other hand, network virtualization has not really enabled the disaggregation of networks envisioned by SDN: the controllers and the switches in a network virtualization system are typically quite tightly integrated using proprietary signalling methods rather than an open interface. And because the focus of network virtualization has been on connecting virtual machines and containers, it is usually implemented as an overlay among the servers on which those computing abstractions are implemented. Sitting underneath that overlay is a physical network, which network virtualization just takes as given (and that physical network need not implement SDN at all).[7] In this book we take a broad view of what SDN is, but at the same time we can see that not all the potential benefits of SDN are delivered by network virtualization.

[7] This observation about different aspects of SDN being implemented in switches versus end hosts is an important one that we return to in Section 3.1.

2.2 Switching Fabrics

The predominant use case for pure play SDN is within cloud datacenters, where for reasons of both lowering costs and improving feature velocity, cloud providers have moved away from proprietary switches (i.e., those traditionally sold by network vendors), in favor of bare-metal switches built using merchant silicon switching chips. These cloud providers then control the *switching fabric* that interconnects their servers entirely in software. This is the use case we explore in-depth throughout this book, so for now we give only a brief introduction.

A datacenter switching fabric is a network often designed according to a *leaf-spine* topology. The basic idea is illustrated by the small 4-rack example shown in Figure 9. Each rack has a *Top-of-Rack (ToR)* switch that interconnects the servers in that rack; these are referred to as the *leaf* switches of the fabric. (There are typically two such ToR switches per rack for resilience, but the figure shows only one for simplicity.) Each leaf switch then connects to a subset of available *spine* switches, with two requirements: (1) that there be multiple paths between any pair of racks, and (2) that each rack-to-rack path is two-hops (i.e., via a single intermediate spine switch). This means in leaf-spine designs like the one shown in Figure 9, every server-to-server path is either two hops (server-leaf-server in the intra-rack case) or four hops (server-leaf-spine-leaf-server in the inter-rack case).

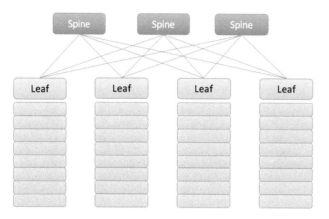

Figure 9: Example of a leaf-spine switching fabric common to cloud datacenters and other compute clusters.

The main fabric-control software sets up L2 forwarding (bridging) within a server-rack, and L3 forwarding (routing) across racks. The use of L3 down-to-the ToR switches is a well-known concept in leaf-spine fabrics, mainly due to L3 scaling better than L2. In such cases, the ToRs (leaves) route traffic by hashing IP flows to different spines using *Equal-Cost Multipath (ECMP)* forwarding. Because every ToR is 2-hops away from every other ToR, there are multiple such equal-cost paths. (Internally, the control software takes advantage of label switching concepts similar to that used by MPLS.) Having the fabric control software also provide L2-bridging comes from the need to support legacy workloads that often expect to communicate over an L2 network. There is much more to implementing a leaf-spine fabric, but we postpone a more complete description until Chapter 7, where we describe the specifics of the Trellis implementation.

2.3 Traffic Engineering for WANs

Another cloud-inspired use case is traffic engineering applied to the wide-area links between datacenters. For example, Google has publicly described their private backbone, called B4, which is built entirely using bare-metal switches and SDN. Similarly, Microsoft has described an approach to interconnecting their data centers called SWAN. A central component of both B4 and SWAN is a *Traffic Engineering (TE)* control program that provisions the network according to the needs of various classes of applications.

The idea of traffic engineering for packet-switched networks is almost as old as packet switching itself, with some ideas of traffic-aware routing having been tried in the Arpanet. However, traffic engineering only really became mainstream for the Internet backbone with the advent of MPLS, which provides a set of tools to steer traffic to balance load across different paths. However, a notable shortcoming of MPLS-based TE is that path calculation, like traditional routing, is a fully distributed process. Central planning tools are common but the real-time management of MPLS paths remains fully distributed. This means that it is near impossible to achieve any sort of global optimization, as the path calculation algorithms–which kick in any time a link changes status, or as traffic loads change–are making local choices about what seems best.

B4 and SWAN recognize this shortcoming and move the path calculation to a logically centralized SDN controller. When a link fails, for example, the controller calculates a new mapping of traffic demands onto available links, and programs the switches to forward traffic flows in such a way that no link is overloaded.

Over many years of operation, these approaches have become more sophisticated. For example, B4 evolved from treating all traffic equally to supporting a range of traffic classes with different levels of tolerance to delay and availability requirements. Examples of traffic classes included: (1) copying user data (e.g., email, documents, audio/video) to remote datacenters for availability; (2) accessing remote storage by computations that run over distributed data sources; and (3) pushing large-scale data to synchronize state across multiple datacenters. In this example, user-data represents the lowest volume on B4, is the most latency sensitive, and is of the highest priority. By breaking traffic up into these classes with different properties, and running a path calculation algorithm for each one, the team was able to considerably improve the efficiency of the network, while still meeting the requirements of the most demanding applications.

Through a combination of centralizing the decision-making process, programmatically rate-limiting traffic at the senders, and differentiating classes of traffic, Google has been able to drive their link utilizations to nearly 100%. This is two to three times better than the 30-40% average utilization that WAN links are typically provisioned for, which is necessary to allow those networks to deal with both traffic bursts and link/switch failures. Microsoft's reported experience with SWAN was similar. These hyperscale experiences with SDN show both the value of being able to customize the network and the power of centralized control to change networking abstractions. A conversation with Amin Vahdat, Jennifer Rexford, and David Clark is especially insightful about the thought process in adopting SDN.

Further Reading:
A. Vahdat, D. Clark, and J. Rexford. A Purpose-built Global Network: Google's Move to SDN. ACM Queue, December 2015.

2.4 Software-Defined WANs

Another use-case for SDN that has taken off for enterprise users is *Software-Defined Wide-Area Networks (SD-WAN)*. Enterprises have for many years been buying WAN services from telecommunications companies, mostly to obtain reliable and private network services to interconnect their many locations–main offices, branch offices, and corporate data centers. For most of the 21st century the most common technical approach to building these networks has been MPLS, using a technique known as MPLS-BGP VPNs (virtual private networks). The rapid rise of SD-WAN as an alternative to MPLS is another example of the power of centralized control.

Provisioning a VPN using MPLS, while less complex than most earlier options, still requires some significant local configuration of both the Customer Edge (CE) router located at each customer site, and the Provider Edge (PE) router to which that site would be connected. In addition, it would typically require the provisioning of a circuit from the customer site to the nearest point of presence for the appropriate Telco.

With SD-WAN, there was a realization that VPNs lend themselves to centralized configuration. An enterprise wants its sites—and only its authorized sites—to be interconnected, and it typically wants to apply a set of policies regarding security, traffic prioritization, access to shared services and so on. These can be input to a central controller, which can then push out all the necessary configuration to a switch located at the appropriate office. Rather than manually configuring a CE and a PE every time a new site is added, it is possible to achieve "zero-touch" provisioning: an appliance is shipped to the new site with nothing more than a certificate and an address to contact, which it then uses to contact the central controller and obtain all the configuration it needs. Changes to policy, which might affect many sites, can be input centrally and pushed out to all affected sites. An example policy would be *"put YouTube traffic into the lowest priority traffic class"* or *"allow direct access to a given cloud service from all branch offices"*. The idea is illustrated in Figure 10.

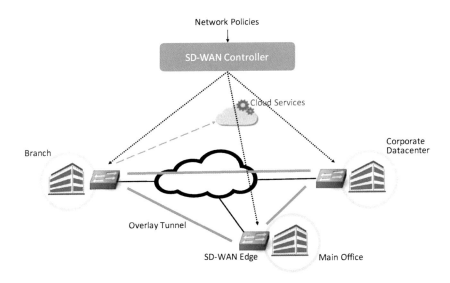

Figure 10: An SD-WAN controller receives policies centrally and pushes them out to edge switches at various sites. The switches build an overlay of tunnels over the Internet or other physical networks, and implement policies including allowing direct access to cloud services.

Note that the "private" part of the VPN is generally achieved by the creation of encrypted tunnels between locations. This is another example of a task that is painful to set up using traditional box-by-box configuration but easy to achieve when all switches are receiving their configuration from a central controller.

Many factors that are external to SDN came into play to make SD-WAN a compelling option. One of these was the ubiquity of broadband Internet access, meaning that there is no longer a reason to provision a dedicated circuit to connect a remote site, with the corresponding time and cost to install. But the privacy issue had to be solved before that could happen—as it was, using centrally managed, encrypted tunnels. Another was the increasing reliance on cloud services such as Office365 or Salesforce.com, which have tended to replace on-premises applications in corporate data centers. It seems natural that you would choose to access those services directly from an Internet-connected branch, but traditional VPNs would *backhaul* traffic to a central site before sending it out to the Internet, precisely so that security could be controlled centrally. With SD-WAN, the central control over security policy is achieved, while the data plane remains fully distributed—meaning that remote sites can directly connect to the cloud services without backhaul. This is yet another example of how separating the control and data planes leads to a new network architecture.

As with some of the other use cases, SD-WAN is not necessarily doing everything that SDN promised. The control plane to data plane communication channel tends to be proprietary, and, like network virtualization, the SD-WAN solutions are overlay networks running on top of traditional networks. Nevertheless, SD-WAN has opened up a path for innovation because both the edge devices and the control planes are implemented in software, and centralization has offered new ways of tackling an old problem. Furthermore, there is plenty of competition among the players in the SD-WAN marketplace.

2.5 Access Networks

Access networks that implement the *last mile* connecting homes, businesses, and mobile devices to the Internet are another opportunity to apply SDN principles. Example access network technologies include

Passive Optical Networks (PON), colloquially known as fiber-to-the-home, and the *Radio Access Network (RAN)* at the heart of the 4G/5G cellular network.

What's interesting about these use cases is that unlike all the others—which effectively open general-purpose switches to programmable control—access networks are typically built from special-purpose hardware devices. The challenge is to transform these purpose-built devices into their merchant silicon/bare-metal counterparts, so they can be controlled by software. In the case of wired networks like PON, there are two such devices: *Optical Line Terminals (OLT)* and *Broadband Network Gateways (BNG)*. In the case of the cellular network, there are also two relevant legacy components: *eNodeB* (the RAN base station) and the *Enhanced Packet Core (EPC)*. A brief introduction is available online if you are not familiar with these acronyms.

Because these devices are purpose-built, not to mention closed and proprietary, they would seem to be worst-case examples for applying SDN principles. But that also means they represent an opportunity for the biggest payoff, and it is for precisely this reason that large network operators are actively pursuing software-defined PON and RAN networks. This initiative is often referred to as *CORD (Central Office Re-architected as a Datacenter)* and has been the subject of much business analysis, including a comprehensive report by A.D. Little.

The central challenge of initiatives like CORD is to disaggregate the existing legacy devices, so as to isolate the underlying packet forwarding engine (the central element of the data plane) from the control plane. Doing so makes it possible to package the former as commodity hardware and to implement the latter in software.

Progress disaggregating PON-based access networks is quite far along, with a solution known as *SEBA (SDN-Enabled Broadband Access)* currently being deployed in operator field trials; production deployments are expected by 2021. Full details are beyond the scope of this book, but the general idea is to add bare-metal OLT devices to a cluster similar to the one presented in Figure 9, resulting in configuration like the one depicted in Figure 11. In other words, the cluster includes a mix of compute servers and access devices, interconnected by a switching fabric. And just as the *Open Compute Project (OCP)*

Further Reading:
Access Networks. *Computer Networks: A Systems Approach*, 2020.

Further Reading:
Who Dares Wins! How Access Transformation Can Fast-Track Evolution of Operator Production Platforms. *A.D. Little Report*, September 2019.

has certified bare-metal ethernet switches, they now also certify bare-metal OLT devices. Both the fabric switches and access devices are controlled by a software-defined control plane, with the code that implements that control plane running on servers in the cluster.

Moreover, when the fabric is constructed using switches with programmable pipelines, certain functionality originally provided by the legacy hardware can be programmed into the switches that comprise the fabric. For example, BNG-equivalent functionality, which could be packaged as a *Virtual Network Function (VNF)* running on a general-purpose processor, is instead programmed directly into a programmable switch. This practice is sometimes called *VNF off-loading* because the packet processing is moved from the compute servers into the switches. This is a great example of what happens when switch data planes become programmable: developers write software that takes advantage of the hardware in new and unanticipated ways.

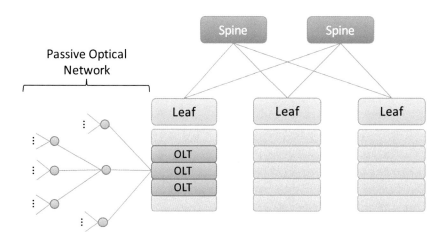

Figure 11: General hardware architecture of SEBA: SDN-Enabled Broadband Access.

Progress on *Software-Defined Radio Access Networks (SD-RAN)* lags software-defined broadband, with development still in the proof-of-concept stage. Disaggregating the RAN is a bigger challenge, but the payoff will likely be even larger, as it leads to a 5G-enabled edge cloud. We revisit SD-RAN in Chapter 8, but for an introduction to how 5G is being implemented according to SDN principles, we recommend a companion book.

Further Reading:
L. Peterson and O. Sunay. 5G Mobile Networks: A Systems Approach. June 2020.

The bottom line is that the effort to apply SDN principles to both fiber and mobile access networks starts with the same building block components described throughout this book. We will highlight where such software-defined access networks "plug into" the SDN software stack as we work our way through the details.

2.6 Network Telemetry

We conclude this overview of SDN use cases by looking at a recent example made possible by the introduction of programmable forwarding pipelines: *In-Band Network Telemetry (INT)*. The idea of INT is to program the forwarding pipeline to collect network state as packets are being processed (i.e., "in-band"). This is in contrast to the conventional monitoring done by the control plane by reading various fixed counters (e.g., packets received/transmitted) or sampling subsets of packets (e.g., sFlow).

In the INT approach, telemetry "instructions" are encoded into packet header fields, and then processed by network switches as they flow through the forwarding pipeline. These instructions tell an INT-capable device what state to collect, and then how to write that state into the packet as it transits the network. INT traffic sources (e.g., applications, end-host networking stacks, hypervisors) can embed the instructions either in normal data packets or in special probe packets. Similarly, INT traffic sinks retrieve and report the collected results of these instructions, allowing the traffic sinks to monitor the exact data plane state that the packets observed (experienced) while being forwarded.

The idea is illustrated in Figure 12, which shows an example packet traversing a path from source switch $S1$ to sink switch $S5$ via transit switch $S2$. The INT metadata added by each switch along the path both indicates what data is to be collected for the packet, and records the corresponding data for each switch.

INT is still early-stage, but it has the potential to provide qualitatively deeper insights into traffic patterns and the root causes of network failures. For example, INT can be used to measure and record queuing delay individual packets experience while traversing a sequence of switches along an end-to-end path, with a packet like the one shown in the figure reporting: *"I visited Switch 1 @780ns, Switch 2 @1.3μs, Switch 5 @2.4μs."* This information can be used, for example, to detect *microbursts*—queuing delays measured over millisecond or even sub-millisecond time scales—as reported by Xiaoqi Chen and colleagues. It is even possible to correlate this information across packet flows that followed different routes, so as to to determine which flows shared buffer capacity at each switch.

Further Reading:
X. Chen, et. al. Fine-grained queue measurement in the data plane. ACM CoNEXT'19, December 2019.

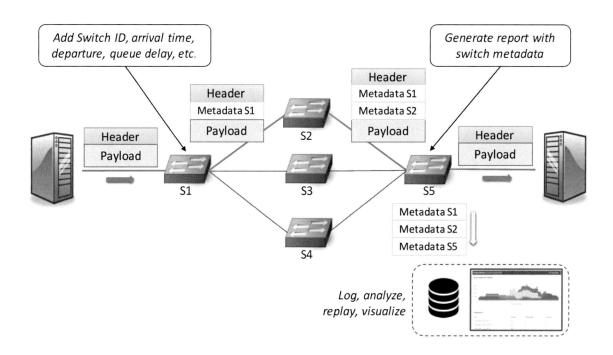

Figure 12: Illustration of Inband Network Telemetry (INT), with each packet collecting measurement data as it traverses the network.

Similarly, packets can report the decision making process that directed their delivery, for example, with something like: *"In Switch 1, I followed rules 75 and 250; in Switch 2, I followed rules 3 and 80."* This opens the door to using INT to verify that the data plane is faithfully executing the forwarding behavior the network operator intended. We return to the potential of INT to impact how we build and operate networks in the concluding chapter of this book.

This use case illustrates once again a potential benefit of SDN: the ability to try out new ideas that would have in the past been infeasible. With traditional fixed-function ASICs doing the packet forwarding, you could never get the chance to try an idea like INT to see if the benefits justify the cost. It is this freedom to experiment and innovate that will lead to lasting benefits from SDN in the long run.

Chapter 3: Basic Architecture

SDN is an approach to building networks that favors programmable commodity hardware, with the intelligence that controls packet forwarding and other network operations implemented in software. Realizing such a design is independent of any particular protocol stack, but instead requires a set of open APIs and a new collection of software components that support those APIs. This chapter introduces the basic architecture of such an *SDN software stack*.

This chapter defines the general architecture of such a software stack, and while there are multiple options for the specific components and tools that can be plugged into this architecture, it also introduces an example set. We do this to make the discussion more concrete, but the particular components we describe have two important attributes. One, they are open source and freely available on GitHub. Two, they are designed to work together, providing a comprehensive solution; there are no gaps in our story. Both attributes make it possible for *anyone* to build the same end-to-end system that is running today in production networks.

3.1 Software Stack

An overview of the software stack is given in Figure 13, which includes a *Bare-Metal Switch* running a local *Switch OS*, controlled by a global Network OS hosting a collection of *Control Applications*. Figure 13 also calls out a corresponding set of exemplar open source components (*Trellis*, *ONOS*, and *Stratum*) on the right, as well as a related *P4 Toolchain* on the left. This chapter introduces these components, with later chapters giving more detail.

Note the similarity between this diagram and Figure 2 in Chapter 1. Both figures include two open interfaces: one between the Control Apps and the Network OS, and a second between the Network OS and the underlying programmable switches. These two interfaces are depicted as "API shims" in Figure 13, and in the context of the exemplar components, correspond to a combination of *gNMI*, *gNOI* and *FlowObjective* in the first case, and a combination of *gNMI*, *gNOI* and either *P4Runtime* or *OpenFlow* in the second case. gRPC is shown as the transport protocol for these APIs—an implementation choice, but one that we will generally assume from here on. (Note that OpenFlow, unlike the other protocols, does not run over gRPC.)

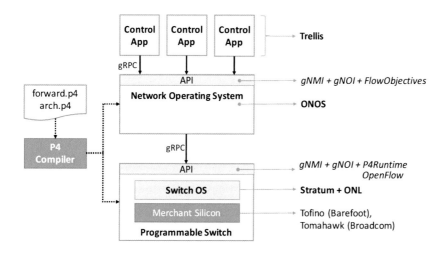

Figure 13: Overall architecture of the SDN software stack.

It is important to keep in mind that the software components listed in Figure 13 correspond to active open source projects, and as a consequence, they continue to evolve (as do their APIs). Specific versions of each component—and their associated APIs—have been integrated and deployed into both trial and production environments. For example, while the figure shows P4Runtime as a candidate control interface exported by the Switch OS, there are deployed solutions that use OpenFlow instead. (This includes the Comcast deployment.) Similarly, while the figure shows gNMI/gNOI as the config/ops interface to each switch, there are solutions that use NETCONF instead.

For the purpose of this book, we do not attempt to track all possible combinations of component versions and APIs, but opt instead to focus on the single consistent stack enumerated in Figure 13, since it represents our best judgement as to the "right" approach based on experience (so far) with earlier versions up-and-down the stack.

3.1.1 Switch vs Host Implementation

The top-to-bottom view of the software stack shown in Figure 13 is from the perspective of a single switch, but it is important to also keep the network perspective in mind. Figure 14 gives such a perspective by focusing on an end-to-end path through the network, connecting Virtual Machines (VMs).

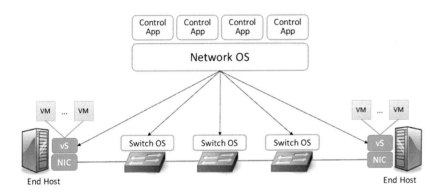

Figure 14: End-to-End Perspective of a Software-Defined Network, including the end hosts and the Virtual Machines (VMs) they host.

This perspective highlights two important aspects of the system. First, it re-enforces that the Network OS (e.g., ONOS) is network-wide, while the Switch OS (e.g., Stratum) is per-switch.

Second, part of the SDN software stack runs on the end hosts. In particular, there is a *Virtual Switch (vSwitch)*—typically implemented in software as part of the hypervisor running on the server—that is responsible for forwarding packets to and from the VMs. (Of course, not every end-host runs VMs, but a similar architecture applies to containers hosts or bare-metal servers). Just like a physical switch, the vSwitch forwards packets from input port to output port, but these are virtual ports connected to VMs (or containers) rather than physical ports connected to physical machines.

Host-Centric Perspective

This book adopts a network-oriented perspective of SDN, one that treats the end-host (both the virtual switch running in the host OS and the NIC connecting the host to the network) as an extension of the network, running under the control of a Network OS. A more host-centric perspective is equally valid, and perhaps more importantly, comes with a robust ecosystem of open source software that runs as part of the host OS.

DPDK is one example, but another gaining traction is the combination of eBPF (extended Berkeley Packet Filter) and XDP (eXpress Data Path). When used together, they provide a way to program generalized Match-Action rules in the OS kernel, or potentially even on a SmartNIC. This is similar in spirit to OpenFlow and P4, except they allow for the Action part to be an arbitrary program. In contrast, OpenFlow defines a fixed set of Actions, and P4 is a restricted language for expressing Actions (e.g., it does not include loops). This is necessary when the Action must execute within a fixed cycle budget, as is the case for a switch-based forwarding pipeline. It also enables formal verification of the data plane, a promising opportunity discussed in Chapter 8.

Fortunately, we can view a vSwitch as behaving just like a physical switch, including the APIs it supports. That a vSwitch is implemented in software on a general-purpose processor rather than in an ASIC is an implementation detail. While this is a true statement, being a software switch dramatically lowers the barrier to introducing additional features, so the feature set is both richer and more dynamic. For example, *Open vSwitch (OVS)* is a widely-used open source vSwitch that supports OpenFlow as a northbound API. It formed the data plane for the original Nicira network virtualization platform. OVS has been integrated with an assortment of complementary tools, such as DPDK (Data Plane Development Kit), another open source component that optimizes packet forwarding operations on x86 processors. Although it's an important topic, this book does not explore the full range of possibilities for a vSwitch like OVS or other end-host optimizations, but instead treats vSwitches just like any other switch along the end-to-end path.

Another implementation detail shown in Figure 14 is that the host may have a *Smart Network Interface Card (SmartNIC)* that assists (or possibly even replaces) the vSwitch. Vendors have a long history of off-loading kernel functionality onto NICs (e.g., everything from computing TCP/IP checksums to supporting VMs), but in the SDN context, the interesting possibility is to replicate the forwarding pipeline found on the network switches. Again, there are a range of possible implementation choices, including both FPGA and ASIC, as well as whether the NIC is fixed-function or programmable (using P4). For our purposes, we will treat such Smart NICs as yet another switching element along the end-to-end path.

3.2 Bare-Metal Switch

Starting at the bottom and working our way up the stack shown in Figures 13 and 14, the network data plane is implemented by an inter-connected set of bare-metal switches. Our focus for now is on a single switch, where the overall network topology is dictated by the Control Applications running at the top of the software stack. For example, we describe a Control Application that manages a leaf-spine topology in a later section.

The architecture is agnostic as to the switch vendor, but the full software stack outlined in this chapter runs on switches built using Tofino and Tomahawk switching chips manufactured by Barefoot Networks (now an Intel company) and Broadcom, respectively. The Tofino chip implements a programmable forwarding pipeline based on PISA, while the Tomahawk chip implements a fixed-function pipeline.

In the case of both chips, a pair of P4 programs defines the forwarding pipeline. The first (forward.p4) specifies the forwarding behavior. The second (arch.p4) specifies the logical architecture of the target forwarding chip. The P4 compiler generates target files that are loaded into both the Network OS and the switch. These target files are not named in Figure 13 (we will return to the details in Chapters 4 and 5), but both components need to know about the output because one *implements* the forwarding behavior (the switch), and the other *controls* the forwarding behavior (the Network OS).

We return to the details of the compiler toolchain in Chapter 4. For now, we will just address the question of why we need a P4 program in the case of a fixed-function switching chip (since we are not using P4 to modify its fixed behavior). The quick summary is that a formal specification of the forwarding pipeline is required to generate the API to the data plane. P4 programs are written to an abstract model of the forwarding pipeline, and whether the chip's actual hardware pipeline is fixed or programmable, we still need to know how to map the abstract pipeline onto the physical pipeline. This is where arch.p4 plays a role. As for the role of forward.p4, this program actually *prescribes* the pipeline in the case of a programmable chip, whereas for the fixed-function chip, forward.p4 merely *describes* the pipeline. But we still need forward.p4 in both cases because the toolchain uses it, along with arch.p4, to generate the API that sits between the control and data planes.

3.3 *Switch OS*

Moving up from the base hardware, each switch runs a local Switch OS. Not to be confused with the Network OS that manages a network of switches, this Switch OS runs on a commodity processor internal to the switch (not shown in Figure 13). It is responsible for handling API calls issued to the switch, for example from the Network OS. This includes taking the appropriate action on the switch's internal resources, which sometimes affects the switching chip.

Multiple open source Switch OSes are available (including SONiC, originally developed at Microsoft Azure), but we use a combination of Stratum and *Open Network Linux (ONL)* as our primary example. ONL is a switch-ready distribution of Linux (originally prepared by Big Switch Networks), while Stratum (originally developed at Google) is primarily responsible for translating between the external-facing API and the internal switch resources. For this reason, we sometimes refer to Stratum as a *Thin Switch OS*.

Stratum mediates all interactions between the switch and the outside world. This includes loading the target files generated by the P4 compiler, which defines a contract between the data plane and the control plane. This contract effectively replaces OpenFlow's flow rule abstraction with an auto-generated specification. The rest of the Stratum-managed API is defined as follows:

- **P4Runtime:** An interface for controlling forwarding behavior at runtime. It is the key for populating forwarding tables and manipulating forwarding state. The P4Runtime is independent of any particular P4 program and agnostic to the underlying hardware. This contrasts to OpenFlow which is rather prescriptive about the forwarding model and how the control plane interacts with it. (For completeness, Figure 13 also lists OpenFlow as an alternative control interface.)

- **gNMI (gRPC Network Management Interface):** Used to set and retrieve configuration state. gNMI is usually paired with OpenConfig YANG models that define the structure of the configuration and state tree.

- **gNOI (gRPC Network Operations Interfaces):** Used to set and retrieve operational state, for example supporting certificates management, device testing, software upgrades, and networking troubleshooting.

If you recall the distinction between Control and Configuration introduced in Chapter 1, then you will recognize P4Runtime as the Control API and the gNMI/gNOI combination as a modern version of a switch's traditional Configuration API. This latter API has historically been called the OAM interface (for "Operations, Administration, and Maintenance"), and it has most often been implemented as a command-line interface (which is of course not really an API).

3.4 Network OS

The Network OS is a platform for configuring and controlling a network of switches. It runs off-switch as a logically centralized SDN controller, and manages a set of switches on a network-wide basis. Central to this role is responsibility for monitoring the state of those switches (e.g., detecting port and link failures), maintaining a global view of the topology that reflects the current state of the network, and making that view available to any interested Control Apps. Those Control Apps, in turn, "instruct" the Network OS to control packet flows through the underlying switches according to whatever service they are providing. The way these "control instructions" are expressed is a key aspect of the Network OS's API.

Going beyond this conceptual description requires a specific Network OS, and we use *ONOS (Open Network Operating System)* as our exemplar. ONOS is best-of-breed in terms of performance, scalability, and availability. At a high-level, ONOS takes responsibility for three things:

- **Managing Topology:** Tracks inventory of network infrastructure devices and their interconnection to provide a shared view of the network environment for the rest of the platform and applications.

- **Managing Configuration:** Facilitates issuing, tracking, rolling back, and validating atomic configuration operations on multiple network devices. This effectively mirrors the per-switch configuration and operation interfaces (also using gNMI and gNOI), but does so at the network level rather than the device level.

- **Controlling Switches:** Controls the data plane packet processing pipelines of the network switches and provides subsequent control of flow rules, groups, meters and other building blocks within those pipelines.

With respect to this last role, ONOS exports a northbound *FlowObjectives* abstraction, which generalizes Flow Rules in a pipeline independent way.[8] This interface, which Chapter 6 describes in more detail, is not standardized in the same way as the control interface exported by individual switches. As with a conventional server OS, applications written to the ONOS API do not easily port to another Network OS. The requirement is that this interface be open and well-defined; not that there be just one such interface. If over time there is

[8] We make no claim that FlowObjectives are an ideal interface for controlling a switch. They evolved out of necessity, allowing developers to deal with different pipelines. Defining a general interface is the subject of ongoing research.

consensus about the Network OS interface, then applications will be more easily portable. But just as with server operating systems, the higher one goes up the software stack, the more difficult it becomes to reach such a consensus.

Finally, although Figure 13 does not show any details about the internals of ONOS, to better appreciate the role it plays in the larger scheme of things, we note that the most critical subsystem in any Network OS is a *Scalable Key/Value Store*. Because ONOS provides a logically centralized view of the network, the key to its performance, scalability, and availability is how it stores that state. In the case of ONOS, this store is provided by a companion open source project, called Atomix, which implements the RAFT consensus algorithm. Storage services like Atomix are the cornerstone of nearly all horizontally scalable cloud services today, as Chapter 6 describes in more detail.

3.5 *Leaf-Spine Fabric*

Because we use ONOS as the Network OS, we are limited to ONOS-hosted SDN Control Applications. For illustrative purposes, we use Trellis as that Control App. Trellis implements a *leaf-spine* fabric on a network of programmable switches. This means Trellis dictates a particular network topology: a leaf-spine topology common to datacenter clusters. As outlined in Section 2.3, this topology includes a set of leaf switches, each of which serves as a Top-of-Rack switch (i.e., it connects all the servers in a single rack), where the leaf switches are, in turn, interconnected by a set of spine switches.

At a high level, Trellis plays three roles. First, it provides a switching fabric that interconnects servers—and the VMs running on those servers—in a multi-rack cluster. Second, it connects the cluster as a whole upstream to peer networks, including the Internet, using BGP (i.e., it behaves much like a router). Third, it connects the cluster as a whole to downstream access networks (i.e., it terminates access network technologies like PON and LTE/5G). In other words, instead of thinking about Trellis as a conventional leaf-spine fabric that's locked away in some datacenter, Trellis is best viewed an interconnect running at the network edge, helping to bridge access-specific edge clouds to IP-based datacenter clouds.

In terms of implementation, Trellis actually corresponds to a suite of Control Apps running on ONOS, as opposed to a single app. This suite supports several control plane features, including:

- VLANs and L2 bridging

- IPv4 and IPv6 unicast and multicast routing

- DHCP L3 relay

- Dual-homing of servers and upstream routers

- QinQ forwarding/termination

- MPLS-based pseudowires.

For each of these features, the corresponding Control App interacts with ONOS—by observing changes in the network topology and issuing Flow Objectives—rather than by using any of the standard protocol implementations found in legacy routers and switches. The only time a legacy protocol is involved is when Trellis needs to communicate with the outside world (e.g., upstream metro/core routers), in which case it uses standard BGP (as implemented by the open source Quagga server). This is actually a common feature of SDN environments: they avoid traditional routing protocols internally, or in a greenfield, but interaction with the outside world still requires them.

Finally, Trellis is sometimes deployed at a single site with multiple mobile base stations connected via Trellis leaf-switches. But Trellis can also be extended to multiple sites deeper into the network using multiple stages of spines, as shown in Figure 15. Chapter 7 describes all of this in more detail.

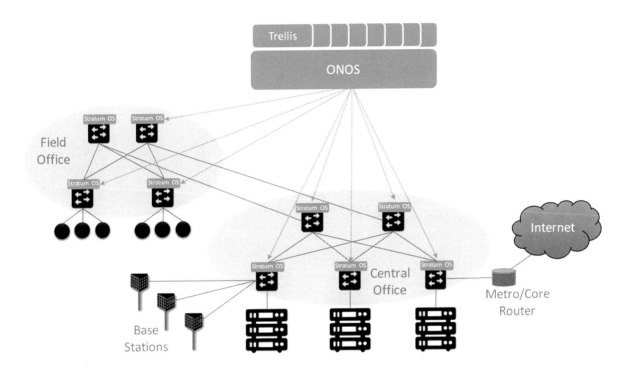

Figure 15: Trellis suite of control apps managing a (potentially distributed) leaf-spine fabric.

Chapter 4: Bare-Metal Switches

This chapter describes the bare-metal switches that provide the underlying hardware foundation for SDN. Our goal is not to give a detailed hardware schematic, but rather, to sketch enough of the design to appreciate the software stack that runs on top of it. Note that this stack is still evolving, with different implementation approaches taken over time and by different vendors. Hence, this chapter discusses both P4 as a language-based approach to programming the switch's data plane, and OpenFlow as the first-generation alternative. We will introduce these two approaches in reverse-chronological order, starting with the more general, programmable case of P4.

4.1 Switch-Level Schematic

We start by considering a bare-metal switch as a whole, where the best analogy is to imagine a PC built from a collection of commodity, off-the-shelf components. In fact, a full architectural specification for switches that take advantage of such components is available on-line at the *Open Compute Project (OCP)*. This is the hardware equivalent of open source software, and makes it possible for anyone to build a high-performance switch, analogous to a home-built PC. But just as the PC ecosystem includes commodity server vendors like Dell and HP, you can buy a pre-built (OCP-compliant) switch from bare-metal switch vendors such as EdgeCore, Delta and others.

Figure 16 gives a high-level schematic of a bare-metal switch. The *Network Processing Unit (NPU)*—a merchant silicon switching chip—is optimized to parse packet headers and make forwarding decisions.

62

NPUs are able to process and forward packets at rates measured in Terabits-per-second (Tbps), easily fast enough to keep up with 32x100-Gbps ports, or the 48x40-Gbps ports shown in the figure. As of this writing, the state-of-the-art for these chips is 25.6 Tbps with 400-Gbps ports.

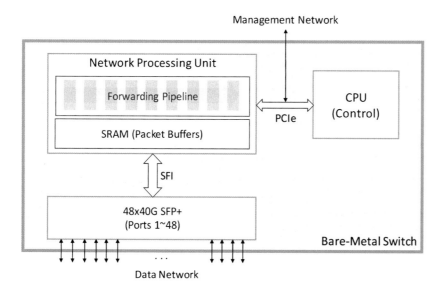

Figure 16: High-Level schematic of a bare-metal switch.

Our use of the term NPU might be considered a bit non-standard. Historically, NPU was the name given to more narrowly-defined network processing chips used, for example, to implement intelligent firewalls or deep packet inspection. They were not as general-purpose as the NPUs we are discussing in this chapter, nor were they as high-performance. The long-term trend, however, has been toward NPUs that match the performance of fixed-function ASICs while providing a much higher degree of flexibility. It seems likely that the current merchant silicon switching chips will make the earlier generation of purpose-built network processors obsolete. The NPU nomenclature used here is consistent with the industry trend to build programmable domain-specific processors, including GPUs (Graphic Processing Units) for graphics and TPUs (Tensor Processing Units) for AI.

Figure 16 shows the NPU as a combination of SRAM-based memory that buffers packets while they are being processed, and an ASIC-based forwarding pipeline that implements a series of (Match, Action) pairs. We describe the forwarding pipeline in more detail in the next section. The switch also includes a general-purpose processor, typically an x86 chip, that controls the NPU. This is where BGP or OSPF would run if the switch is configured to support an on-switch control plane, but for our purposes, it's where the Switch OS runs, exporting an API that allows an off-switch, Network OS to control the data plane. This control processor communicates with the NPU, and is connected to an external management network, over a standard PCIe bus.

Figure 16 also shows other commodity components that make this all practical. In particular, it is possible to buy pluggable transceiver modules that take care of all the media access details—be it 40-Gigabit Ethernet, 10-Gigabit PON, or SONET—as well as the optics. These transceivers all conform to standardized form factors, such as SFP+, that can in turn be connected to other components over a standardized bus (e.g., SFI). Again, the key takeaway is that the networking industry is now entering into the same commoditized world that the computing industry has enjoyed for the last two decades.

Finally, although not shown in Figure 16, each switch includes a BIOS, which much like its microprocessor counterpart, is firmware that provisions and boots a bare-metal switch. A standard BIOS called the *Open Network Install Environment (ONIE)* has emerged under the OCP's stewardship, and so we assume ONIE throughout the rest of the chapter.

4.2 Forwarding Pipeline

High-speed switches use a multi-stage pipeline to process packets. The relevance of using a multi-stage pipeline rather than a single-stage processor is that forwarding a single packet likely involves looking at multiple header fields. Each stage can be programmed to look at a different combination of fields. A multi-stage pipeline adds a little end-to-end latency to each packet (measured in nanoseconds), but means that multiple packets can be processed at the same time. For example, Stage 2 can be making a second lookup on packet A while

Stage 1 is doing an initial lookup on packet B, and so on. This means the pipeline as a whole is able to keep up with the aggregate bandwidth of all its input ports. Repeating the numbers from the previous section, the state-of-the-art is currently 25.6 Tbps.

The main distinction in how a given NPU implements this pipeline is whether the stages are fixed-function (i.e., each stage understands how to process headers for some fixed protocol) or programmable (i.e., each stage is dynamically programmed to know what header fields to process). In the following discussion we start with the more general case—a programmable pipeline—and return to its fixed-function counterpart at the end.

At an architectural level, the programmable pipeline is often referred to as a *Protocol Independent Switching Architecture (PISA)*. Figure 17 gives a high-level overview of PISA, which includes three major components. The first is a *Parser*, which is programmed to define what header fields (and their location in the packet) are to be recognized and matched by later stages. The second is a sequence of *Match-Action Units*, each of which is programmed to match (and potentially act upon) one or more of the identified header fields. The third is the *Deparser*, which re-serializes the packet metadata into the packet before it is transmitted on the output link. The deparser reconstructs the over-the-wire representation for each packet from all the in-memory header fields processed by earlier stages.

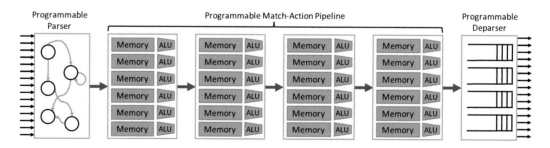

Not shown in the figure is a collection of metadata about the packets traversing the pipeline. This includes both per-packet state, such as the input port and arrival timestamp, and flow-level state computed across successive packets, such as switch counters and queue depth.

Figure 17: High-level overview of PISA's multi-stage pipeline.

This metadata, which has an ASIC counterpart (e.g., a register), is available for individual stages to read and write. It can also be used by the Match-Action Unit, for example matching on the input port.

The individual Match-Action Units in Figure 17 deserve a closer look. The memory shown in the figure is typically built using a combination of SRAM and TCAM: it implements a table that stores bit patterns to be matched in the packets being processed. The relevance of the specific combination of memories is that TCAM is more expensive and power-hungry than SRAM, but it is able to support wildcard matches. Specifically, the "CAM" in TCAM stands for "Content Addressable Memory," which means that the key you want to look up in a table can effectively be used as the address into the memory that implements the table. The "T" stands for "Ternary" which is a technical way to say the key you want to look up can have wildcards in it (e.g., key 10*1 matches both 1001 and 1011). From the software perspective, the main takeaway is that wildcard matches are more expensive than exact matches, and should be avoided when possible.

The ALU shown in the figure then implements the action paired with the corresponding pattern. Possible actions include modifying specific header fields (e.g., decrementing a TTL), pushing or popping tags (e.g., VLAN, MPLS), incrementing or clearing counters internal to the switch (e.g., packets processed), and setting user/internal metadata (e.g. the VRF ID to be used in the routing table).

Directly programming the parser, match-action units, and deparser would be tedious, akin to writing microprocessor assembly code, so instead we express the desired behavior using a high-level language like P4, and depend on a compiler to generate the equivalent low-level program. We will get to the specifics of P4 in a later section, so for now we substitute an even more abstract representation of the desired forwarding pipeline: the graphical depiction included in Figure 18. (To be consistent with other examples, we call this program forward.p4.) This example program first matches L2 header fields, then matches either IPv4 or IPv6 header fields, and finally applies some ACL rules to the packets before allowing them through (e.g., think of the latter as firewall filter rules). This is an example of the OpenFlow pipeline shown in Figure 7 of Section 1.2.3.

In addition to translating the high-level representation of the pipeline onto the underlying PISA stages, the P4 compiler is also responsible for allocating the available PISA resources. In this case, there are four slots (rows) for the available Match-Action Units just as in Figure 17. Allocating slots in the available Match-Action units is the P4/PISA counterpart of register allocation for a conventional programming language running on a general-purpose microprocessor. In our example, we assume there are many more IPv4 Match-Action rules than IPv6 or ACL rules, so the compiler allocates entries in the available Match-Action Units accordingly.

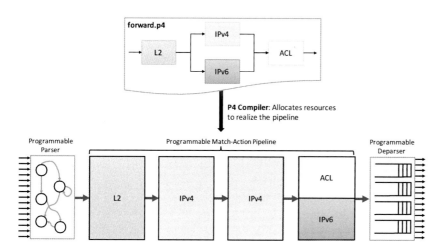

Figure 18: Depiction of the desired forwarding behavior (as specified by a pictorial representation of a P4 program) mapped onto PISA.

4.3 Abstracting the Pipeline

The next piece of the puzzle is to account for different switching chips implementing different physical pipelines. To do this we need an abstract (canonical) pipeline that is general enough to fairly represent the available hardware, plus a definition of how the abstract pipeline maps onto the physical pipeline. With such a logical model for the pipeline, we will be able to support pipeline-agnostic controllers, as illustrated in Figure 19.

Ideally, there will be just one logical pipeline, and the P4 compiler will be responsible for mapping that logical pipeline into various physical counterparts. Unfortunately, the marketplace has not yet converged on a single logical pipeline, but let's put that complication aside for now. On the other side of the equation, there are currently on the order of ten target ASICs that this approach needs to account for. There are many more than ten switch vendors, but in practice, it is only those built for the high-end of the market that come into play.

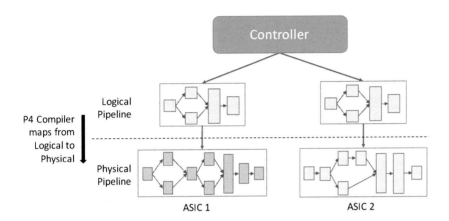

Figure 19: Defining a logical pipeline as a general approach to supporting a pipeline-agnostic control plane.

How do we specify the logical pipeline? This is also done with a P4 program, resulting in the situation shown in Figure 20. Notice that we are revisiting the two P4 programs introduced in Figure 13. The first (forward.p4) defines the functionality we want from the available switching chip. This program is written by the developers who want to establish the behavior of the data plane. The second program (arch.p4) is essentially a header file: it represents a contract between the P4 program and the P4 compiler. Specifically, arch.p4 defines what P4-programmable blocks are available, the interface for each stage, and the capability for each stage. Who is responsible for writing such an architecture program? The P4 Consortium is one source, but different switch vendors have created their own architecture specifications to closely describe the capabilities of their switching chips. This makes sense because there is a tension between having a single common architecture that enables executing the same P4 program on different ASICs from different vendors, and having an architecture that best represents the differentiating capabilities of any given ASIC.

The example shown in Figure 20 is called the *Portable Switch Architecture (PSA)*. It is intended to provide P4 developers implementing forwarding programs like forward.p4 with an abstract target machine, analogous to a Java Virtual Machine. The goal is the same as for Java: to support a *write-once-run-anywhere* programming paradigm. (Note that Figure 20 includes the generic arch.p4 as the architecture model spec, but in practice the architecture model would PSA specific, such as psa.p4.)

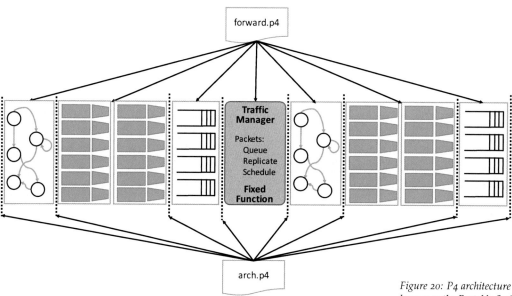

Figure 20: *P4 architecture known as the Portable Switch Architecture (PSA). Includes the generic* arch.p4 *as the architecture model spec, but for PSA this would be replaced by* psa.p4.

When compared to the simpler PISA model used in Figure 17 and 18, we see two major differences. First, the pipeline includes a new fixed-function stage: the *Traffic Manager*. This stage is responsible for queuing, replicating, and scheduling packets. This stage can be configured in well-defined ways (e.g., setting parameters such as queue size and scheduling policy), but cannot be re-programmed in a general-purpose way (e.g., to define a new scheduling algorithm). Second, the pipeline is divided into two halves: *ingress processing* (to the left of the Traffic Manager), and *egress processing* (to the right of the Traffic Manager).

What exactly does arch.p4 define? Essentially three things:

1. As implied by Figure 20, it defines the inter-block interface signatures in terms of input and output signals (think "function parameters and return type"). The goal of a P4 programmer to provide an implementation for each P4-programmable block that takes the provided input signals, such as the input port where a packet was received, and writes to the output signals to influence the behavior of the following blocks (e.g., the output queue/port where a packet has to be directed).

2. Type declarations for *externs*, which can be seen as additional fixed-function services that are exposed by the target and which can be invoked by a P4 programmer. Examples of such externs are checksum and hash computation units, packet or byte counters, ciphers to encrypt/decrypt the packet payload, and so on. The implementation of such externs is *not* specified in P4 by the architecture, but their interface is.

3. Extensions to core P4 language types, including alternative match types (e.g., range and lpm described in Section 4.4.3).

The P4 compiler (like all compilers) has a hardware-agnostic *frontend* that generates an *Abstract Syntax Tree (AST)* for the programs being compiled, and a hardware-specific *backend* that outputs an ASIC-specific executable. arch.p4 is simply a collection of type and interface definitions.

4.3.1 V1Model

The PSA shown in Figure 20 is still a work-in-progress. It represents an idealized architecture that sits between the P4 developer and the underlying hardware, but the architectural model that developers are coding to today is somewhat simpler. That model, called V1Model, is shown in Figure 21.[9] It does not include a re-parsing step after the Traffic Manager. Instead it implicitly bridges all metadata from ingress to egress processing. Also, V1Model includes a checksum verification/update block, whereas PSA treats checksums as an ex-

[9] V1Model was originally introduced as the reference architecture for an earlier version of P4, known as P4_14, and was subsequently used to ease the porting of P4 programs from P4_14 to P4_16.

tern, and supports incremental computations at any point during ingress/egress processing.

We will be using this simpler model throughout the rest of the book. As an aside, the most important factor in why V1Model is widely used and that is not the case for PSA, is that the switch vendors do not provide the compiler backend that maps from PSA onto their respective ASICs. Until that happens, PSA will remain a mostly "on paper" artifact.

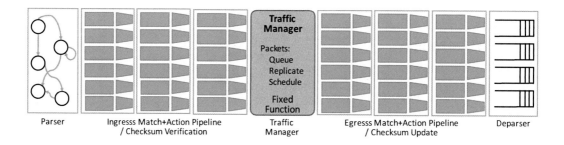

| Parser | Ingress Match+Action Pipeline / Checksum Verification | Traffic Manager | Egress Match+Action Pipeline / Checksum Update | Deparser |

Figure 21: V1Model used in practice to abstract away the details of different physical forwarding pipelines. Developers write P4 to this abstract architectural model.

When we say P4 developers "write to this model" we are being more descriptive than you might think. In practice, every P4 program starts with the following template, which literally has a code block for every programmable element in the abstract depiction shown in Figure 21.

That is, after including two definition files (core.p4, v1model.p4) and defining the packet headers that the pipeline is going to process, the programmer writes P4 code blocks for parsing, checksum verification, ingress processing, and so on. The final block (V1Switch) is the "main" function that specifies all the pieces are to be pulled together into a complete switch pipeline. As to the details corresponding to every "…" in the template, we will return to those in a later section. For now, the important point is that forward.p4 is a highly stylized program that gets its structure from the abstract model defined in v1model.p4.

```
#include <core.p4>
#include <v1model.p4>

/* Headers */
struct metadata { ... }
struct headers {
        ethernet_t         ethernet;
        ipv4_t                  ipv4;
}

/* Parser */
parser MyParser(
        packet_in packet,
        out headers hdr,
        inout metadata meta,
        inout standard_metadata_t smeta) {
    ...
}

/* Checksum Verification */
control MyVerifyChecksum(
        in headers, hdr,
        inout metadata meta) {
    ...
}

/* Ingress Proceessing */
control MyIngress(
        inout headers hdr,
        inout metadata meta,
        inout standard_metadata_t smeta) {
    ...
}

/* Egress Proceessing */
control MyEgress(
        inout headers hdr,
        inout metadata meta,
        inout standard_metadata_t smeta) {
    ...
}
```

```
/* Checksum Update */
control MyComputeChecksum(
        inout headers, hdr,
        inout metadata meta) {
    ...
}

/* Deparser */
parser MyDeparser(
        inout headers hdr,
        inout metadata meta) {
    ...
}

/* Switch */
V1Switch(
    MyParser(),
    MyVerifyChecksum(),
    MyIngress(),
    MyEgress(),
    MyComputeChecksum(),
    MyDeparser()
) main;
```

4.3.2 TNA

As just noted, V1Model is one of many possible pipeline architectures. PSA is another, but it is also the case that different switch vendors have provided their own architecture definitions. There are different incentives for doing this. One is that vendors have their own version of the multi-ASIC problem as they continue to release new chips over time. Another is that it enables vendors to expose unique capabilities of their ASICs without being constrained by a standardization process. The *Tofino Native Architecture (TNA)*, which is an architecture model defined by Barefoot for their family of programmable switching chips, is an example.

We do not give this example because we plan to define TNA, but rather, because having a second tangible example helps to illustrate all the degrees of freedom available in this space. In effect, the P4 language defines a general framework for writing programs (we'll see the syntax in the next section), but it's not until you supply a P4 architecture definition (generically we refer to this as arch.p4, but specific examples are v1model.p4, psa.p4, and tna.p4) that a developer is able to actually write and compile a forwarding program.

In contrast to v1model.p4 and psa.p4, which aspire to abstracting commonality across different switching chips, architectures like tna.p4 faithfully define the low-level capabilities of a given chip. Often, such capabilities are those that differentiate a chip like Tofino from the competition (For this reason, the definition of such vendor/chip-specific architectures is not public and often requires signing a non-disclosure agreement.) When picking an architecture model for a new P4 program, it is important to ask questions like: Which of the available architectures are supported by the switches I intend to program? Does my program need access to chip-specific capabilities (e.g., a P4 extern to encrypt/decrypt packet payload) or can it rely solely on common/non-differentiating features (e.g., simple match-action tables or a P4 extern to count packets)? Do I want the P4 program I develop to be public on GitHub?

As for that forwarding program (which we've been generically referring to as forward.p4), an interesting tangible example is a program that faithfully implements all the features that a conventional L2/L3 switch supports. Let's call that program switch.p4.[10] Strangely enough, that leaves us having re-created the legacy switch we could have bought from dozens of vendors, but there are two notable differences: (1) we can control that switch using an SDN controller via P4Runtime, and (2) we can easily modify that program should we discover we need a new feature.

Is the Complexity Worth It?

At this point you may be wondering if all the complexity being introduced is worth it, and we haven't even gotten to the control plane yet! What we've covered so far is complex with or without SDN. That's because we're working at the SW/HW boundary, and the hard-

[10] Such a program exists (it was written by Barefoot for their chipset and uses tna.p4 as its architecture model), but it is not open source. A roughly equivalent open source variant, called fabric.p4, uses v1model.p4, but it is more narrowly written to support Trellis (see Chapter 7) than serving as a general-purpose L2/L3 data plane.

ware is designed to forward packets at rates measured in Terabits-per-second. This complexity use to be hidden inside proprietary devices. All that SDN has done is put pressure on the marketplace to open up that space so others can innovate.

But before anyone can innovate, the first step is to reproduce what we had running before, except now using open interfaces and programmable hardware. Even though this chapter uses forward.p4 *as a hypothetical new data plane function someone might write, it's really programs like* switch.p4 *(plus the Switch OS described in the next chapter) that establish parity with legacy networking gear. Once we have that in place, we are ready to do something new. But what?*

It is not our goal to answer that question with any certainty. The VNF off-loading and INT examples introduced in Chapter 2 are a start. Chapter 8 goes on to introduce closed-loop verification and software-defined 5G networks as potential killer-apps. But history teaches us that killer-apps are impossible to predict with any accuracy. On the other hand, history also includes many examples of how opening closed, fixed-function systems leads to qualitatively new capabilities.

To summarize, the overarching goal is to enable the development of control apps without regard to the specific details of the device forwarding pipeline. Introducing the P4 architecture model helps meet this goal, as it enables portability of the same forwarding pipeline (P4 program) across multiple targets (switching chips) that support the corresponding architecture model. However, it doesn't totally solve the problem because the industry is still free to define multiple forwarding pipelines. But looking beyond the current state-of-affairs, having one or more programmable switches opens the door to programming the control app(s) and the forwarding pipeline in tandem. When everything is programmable, all the way down to the chip that forwards packets in the data plane, exposing that programmability to developers is the ultimate goal. If you have an innovative new function you want to inject into the network, you write both the control plane and data plane halves of that function, and turn the crank on the toolchain to load them into the SDN software stack! This is a significant step forward from a few years ago, where you might have been able to modify a routing protocol (because it was all in software) but you had no chance to change the forwarding pipeline because it was all in fixed-function hardware.

4.4 P4 Programs

Finally, we give a brief overview of the P4 language. The following is not a comprehensive reference manual for P4. Our more modest goal is to give a sense of what a P4 program looks like, thereby connecting all the dots introduced up to this point. We do this by example, that is, by walking through a P4 program that implements basic IP forwarding. This example is taken from a P4 Tutorial that you can find online and try for yourself.

To help set some context, think of P4 as similar to the C programming language. P4 and C share a similar syntax, which makes sense because both are designed for low-level systems code. Unlike C, however, P4 does not include loops, pointers, or dynamic memory allocation. The lack of loops makes sense when you remember that we are specifying what happens in a single pipeline stage. In effect, P4 "unrolls" the loops we might otherwise need, implementing each iteration in one of a sequence of control blocks (i.e., stages). In the example program that follows, you can imagine plugging each code block into the template shown in the previous section.

Further Reading:
P4 Tutorials. P4 Consortium, May 2019.

4.4.1 Header Declarations and Metadata

First comes the protocol header declarations, which for our simple example includes the Ethernet and IP headers. This is also a place to define any program-specific metadata we want to associate with the packet being processed. The example leaves this structure empty, but v1model.p4 defines a standard metadata structure for the architecture as a whole. Although not shown in the following code block, this standard metadata structure includes such fields as ingress_port (port the packet arrived on), egress_port (port selected to send the packet out on), and drop (bit set to indicate the packet is to be dropped). These fields can be read or written by the rest of the program.[11]

[11] A quirk of the V1Model is that there are two egress port fields in the metadata structure. One (egress_port) is read-only and valid only in the egress processing stage. A second (egress_spec), is the field that gets written from the ingress processing stage to pick the output port. PSA and other architectures solve this problem by defining different metadata for the ingress and egress pipelines.

```
#include <core.p4>
#include <v1model.p4>

const bit<16> TYPE_IPV4 = 0x800;


/*****************************************************
************** H E A D E R S  ************************
*****************************************************/

typedef bit<9>  egressSpec_t;
typedef bit<48> macAddr_t;
typedef bit<32> ip4Addr_t;

header ethernet_t {
    macAddr_t dstAddr;
    macAddr_t srcAddr;
    bit<16>   etherType;
}

header ipv4_t {
    bit<4>     version;
    bit<4>     ihl;
    bit<8>     diffserv;
    bit<16>    totalLen;
    bit<16>    identification;
    bit<3>     flags;
    bit<13>    fragOffset;
    bit<8>     ttl;
    bit<8>     protocol;
    bit<16>    hdrChecksum;
    ip4Addr_t srcAddr;
    ip4Addr_t dstAddr;
}

struct metadata { /* empty */ }

struct headers {
    ethernet_t   ethernet;
    ipv4_t       ipv4;
}
```

4.4.2 Parser

The next block implements the parser. The underlying programming model for the parser is a state transition diagram, including the built-in start, accept, and reject states. The programmer adds other states (parse_ethernet and parse_ipv4 in our example), plus the state transition logic. For example, the following parser always transitions from the start state to the parse_ethernet state, and if it finds the TYPE_IPV4 (see the constant definition in the previous code block) in the etherType field of the Ethernet header, next transitions to the parse_ipv4 state. As a side-effect of traversing each state, the corresponding header is extracted from the packet. The values in these in-memory structures are then available to the other routines, as we will see below.

```
/*************************************************
************* P A R S E R  *************************
*************************************************/

parser MyParser(
        packet_in packet, out headers hdr,
        inout metadata meta,
        inout standard_metadata_t standard_metadata) {

    state start {
        transition parse_ethernet;
    }

    state parse_ethernet {
        packet.extract(hdr.ethernet);
        transition select(hdr.ethernet.etherType) {
            TYPE_IPV4: parse_ipv4;
            default: accept;
        }
    }

    state parse_ipv4 {
        packet.extract(hdr.ipv4);
        transition accept;
    }
}
```

As is the case with all the code blocks in this section, the function signature for the parser is defined by the architecture model, in this case, v1model.p4. We do not comment further on the specific parameters, except to make the general observation that P4 is architecture-agnostic. The program you write depends heavily on the architecture model you include.

4.4.3 Ingress Processing

Ingress processing has two parts. The first is checksum verification.[12] This is minimal in our example; it simply applies the default. The interesting new feature this example introduces is the control construct, which is effectively P4's version of a procedure call. While it is possible for a programmer to also define "subroutines" as their sense of modularity dictates, at the top level these control blocks match up one-for-one with the pipeline stages defined by the logical pipeline model.

[12] This is particular to V1Model. PSA doesn't have an explicit checksum verification or computation stage of ingress or egress respectively.

```
/****************************************************
*** C H E C K S U M    V E R I F I C A T I O N   ***
****************************************************/

control MyVerifyChecksum(
        inout headers hdr,
        inout metadata meta) {
    apply {  }
}
```

We now get to the heart of the forwarding algorithm, which is implemented in the ingress segment of the Match-Action pipeline. What we find are two actions being defined: drop() and ipv4_foward(). The second of these two is the interesting one. It takes a dstAddr and an egress port as arguments, assigns the port to the corresponding field in the standard metadata structure, sets the srcAddr/dstAddr fields in the packet's ethernet header, and decrements the ttl field of the IP header. After executing this action, the headers and metadata associated with this packet contain enough information to properly carry out the forwarding decision.

But how does that decision get made? This is the purpose of the table construct. The table definition includes a key to be looked up, a possible set of actions (ipv4_forward, drop, NoAction), the size of the table (1024 entries), and the default action to take whenever there is no match in the table (drop). The key specification includes both the header field to be looked up (the dstAddr field of the IPv4 header), and the type of match we want (lpm implies Longest Prefix Match). Other possible match types include exact and ternary, the latter of which effectively applies a mask to select which bits in the key to include in the comparison. lpm, exact and ternary are part of the core P4 language types, where their definitions can be found in core.p4. P4 architectures can expose additional match types. For example, PSA also defines range and selector matches.

The final step of the ingress routine is to "apply" the table we just defined. This is done only if the parser (or previous pipeline strage) marked the IP header as valid.

```
/*****************************************************
****** I N G R E S S    P R O C E S S I N G   *******
*****************************************************/

control MyIngress(
        inout headers hdr,
        inout metadata meta,
        inout standard_metadata_t standard_metadata) {

    action drop() {
        mark_to_drop(standard_metadata);
    }

    action ipv4_forward(macAddr_t dstAddr,
                          egressSpec_t port) {
        standard_metadata.egress_spec = port;
        hdr.ethernet.srcAddr = hdr.ethernet.dstAddr;
        hdr.ethernet.dstAddr = dstAddr;
        hdr.ipv4.ttl = hdr.ipv4.ttl - 1;
    }
```

```
    table ipv4_lpm {
        key = {
            hdr.ipv4.dstAddr: lpm;
        }
        actions = {
            ipv4_forward;
            drop;
            NoAction;
        }
        size = 1024;
       default_action = drop();
    }

    apply {
        if (hdr.ipv4.isValid()) {
            ipv4_lpm.apply();
        }
    }
}
```

4.4.4 Egress Processing

Egress processing is a no-op in our simple example, but in general it is an opportunity to perform actions based on the egress port, which might not be known during ingress processing (e.g., it might depend on the traffic manager). For example, replicating a packet to multiple egress ports for multicast can be done by setting the corresponding intrinsic metadata in the ingress processing, where the meaning of such metadata is defined by the architecture. The egress processing will see as many copies of the same packet as those generated by the traffic manager. As a second example, if one switch port is expected to send VLAN-tagged packets, the header must be extended with the VLAN id. A simple way of dealing with such a scenario is by creating a table that matches on the egress_port of the ingress metadata. Other examples include ingress port pruning for multicast packets and adding a "CPU header" for intercepted packets passed to the control plane.

```
/**************************************************
******* E G R E S S   P R O C E S S I N G   ********
**************************************************/

control MyEgress(
        inout headers hdr,
        inout metadata meta,
        inout standard_metadata_t standard_metadata) {

    apply {  }
}

/**************************************************
*** C H E C K S U M   C O M P U T A T I O N  ****
**************************************************/

control MyComputeChecksum(
        inout headers  hdr,
        inout metadata meta) {

    apply {
        update_checksum(
            hdr.ipv4.isValid(),
              { hdr.ipv4.version,
                hdr.ipv4.ihl,
                hdr.ipv4.diffserv,
                hdr.ipv4.totalLen,
                hdr.ipv4.identification,
                hdr.ipv4.flags,
                hdr.ipv4.fragOffset,
                hdr.ipv4.ttl,
                hdr.ipv4.protocol,
                hdr.ipv4.srcAddr,
                hdr.ipv4.dstAddr },
            hdr.ipv4.hdrChecksum,
            HashAlgorithm.csum16);
    }
}
```

4.4.5 *Deparser*

The deparser is typically straightforward. Having potentially changed various header fields during packet processing, we now have an opportunity to emit the updated header fields. If you change a header in one of your pipeline stages, you need to remember to emit it. Only headers that are marketed as valid will be re-serialized into that packet. There is no need to say anything about the rest of the packet (i.e., the payload), since by default, all the bytes beyond where we stopped parsing are included in the outgoing message. The details of how packets are emitted are specified by the architecture. For example, TNA supports truncating the payload based on the setting of a special metadata value consumed by the deparser.

```
/*****************************************************
************** D E P A R S E R *********************
*****************************************************/

control MyDeparser(
        packet_out packet,
        in headers hdr) {

    apply {
        packet.emit(hdr.ethernet);
        packet.emit(hdr.ipv4);
    }
}
```

4.4.6 *Switch Definition*

Finally, the P4 program must define the behavior of the switch as a whole, which is given by the V1Switch package shown below. This set of elements in this package is defined by v1model.p4, and consists of references to all the other routines defined above.

   Keep in mind this example is minimal, but it does serve to illustrate the essential ideas in a P4 program. What's hidden by this example is the interface used by the control plane to inject data into the routing table; table ipv4_lpm defines the table, but does not populate it with

```
/*****************************************************
************* S W I T C H *************************
*****************************************************/

V1Switch(
    MyParser(),
    MyVerifyChecksum(),
    MyIngress(),
    MyEgress(),
    MyComputeChecksum(),
    MyDeparser()
) main;
```

values. We resolve the mystery of how the control plane puts values into the table when we discuss P4Runtime in Chapter 5.

4.5 Fixed-Function Pipelines

We now return to fixed-function forwarding pipelines, with the goal of placing them in the larger ecosystem. Keeping in mind that fixed-function switching chips still dominate the market, we do not mean to understate their value or the role they will undoubtedly continue to play.[13] But they do remove one degree-of-freedom—the ability to re-program the data plane—which helps to highlight the the relationship between all the moving parts introduced in this chapter.

4.5.1 OF-DPA

We start with a concrete example: The *OpenFlow—Data Plane Abstraction (OF-DPA)* hardware abstraction layer that Broadcom provides for their switching chips. OF-DPA defines an API that can be used to install flow rules into the underlying Broadcom ASIC. Technically, an OpenFlow agent sits on top of OF-DPA (it implements the over-the-wire aspects of the OpenFlow protocol) and the Broadcom SDK sits below OF-DPA (it implements the proprietary interface that knows

[13] The distinction between fixed-function and pro-grammable pipelines is not as black-and-white as this discussion implies, since fixed-function pipelines can also be configured. But parameterizing a switching chip and programming a switching chip are qualitatively different, with only the latter able to accommodate new functionality.

about the low-level chip details), but OF-DPA is the layer that provides an abstract representation of the Tomahawk ASIC's fixed forwarding pipeline. Figure 22 shows the resulting software stack, where OF-Agent and OF-DPA are open source (the OF-Agent corresponds to a software module called Indigo, originally written by Big Switch), whereas the Broadcom SDK is proprietary. Figure 23 then depicts what the OF-DPA pipeline looks like.

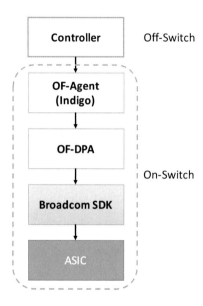

Figure 22: Software stack for Tomahawk fixed-function forwarding pipeline.

We do not delve into the details of Figure 23, but the reader will recognize tables for several well-known protocols. For our purposes, what is instructive is to see how OF-DPA maps onto its programmable pipeline counterparts. In the programmable case, it's not until you add a program like switch.p4 that you get something roughly equivalent OF-DPA. That is, v1model.p4 defines the available stages (control blocks). It's not until you add switch.p4 that you have the functionality that runs in those stages.

With this relationship in mind, we might want to incorporate both programmable and fixed-function switches in a single network and running a common SDN software stack. This can be accomplished by hiding both types of chips behind the v1model.p4 (or similar) architecture model, and letting the P4 compiler output the backend code understood by their respective SDKs. Obviously this scenario doesn't

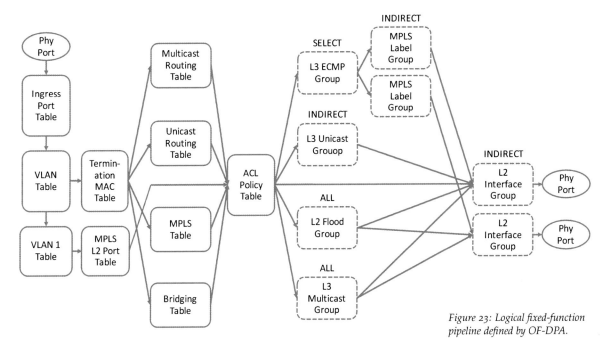

Figure 23: Logical fixed-function pipeline defined by OF-DPA.

work for an arbitrary P4 program that wants to do something that the Tomahawk chip doesn't support, but it will work for standard L2/L3 switch behavior.

4.5.2 SAI

Just as we saw both vendor-defined and community-defined architecture models (TNA and V1Model, respectively), there are also vendor-defined and community-defined logical fixed-function pipelines. OF-DPA is the former, and the *Switch Abstraction Interface (SAI)* is an example of the latter. Because SAI has to work across a range of switches—and forwarding pipelines—it necessarily focuses on the subset of functionality all vendors can agree on, the least common denominator, so to speak.

SAI includes both a configuration interface and a control interface,

where its the control interface that's most relevant to this section because it abstracts the forwarding pipeline. On the other hand, there
is little value in looking at yet another forwarding pipeline, so we refer the interested reader to the SAI specification for more details. We
revisit the configuration API in the next chapter.

Further Reading:
SAI Pipeline Behavioral Model.
Open Compute Project.

4.6 Comparison

This discussion about logical pipelines and their relationship to P4
programs is subtle, and worth restating. On the one hand, there is obvious value in having an abstract representation of a physical pipeline,
as introduced as a general concept in Figure 19. When used in this
way, a logical pipeline is an example of the tried-and-true idea of
introducing a hardware abstraction layer. In our case, it helps with
control plane portability. OF-DPA is a specific example of a hardware
abstraction layer for Broadcom's fixed-function switching chips.

On the other hand, P4 provides a programming model, with architectures like v1model.p4 and tna.p4 adding detail to P4's general
language constructs (e.g., control, table, parser). These architecture models are, in effect, a language-based abstraction of a generic forwarding
device, which can be fully-resolved into a logical pipeline by adding
a particular P4 program like switch.p4. P4 architecture models don't
define pipelines of match-action tables, but they instead define the
building blocks (including signatures) that can be used by a P4 developer to define a pipeline, whether logical or physical. In a sense,
then, P4 architectures are equivalent to a traditional switch SDK, as
illustrated by the five side-by-side examples in Figure 24.

Each example in Figure 24 consists of three layers: a switching
chip ASIC, a vendor-specific SDK for programming the ASIC, and a
definition of the forwarding pipeline. By providing a programmatic
interface, the SDKs in the middle layer effectively abstract the underlying hardware. They are either conventional (e.g., the Broadcom
SDK shown in the second and fourth examples) or as just pointed out,
logically corresponds to a P4 architecture model paired with an ASIC-
specific P4 compiler. The topmost layer in all five examples defines a
logical pipeline that can subsequently be controlled using a control

interface like OpenFlow or P4Runtime (not shown). The five examples differ based on whether the pipeline is defined by a P4 program or through some other means (e.g., the OF-DPA specification).

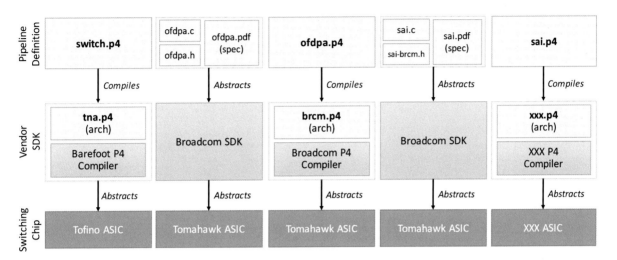

Note that only those configurations with a P4-defined logical pipeline at the top of the stack (i.e., first, third, fifth examples) can be controlled using P4Runtime. This is for the pragmatic reason that the P4Runtime interface is auto-generated from this P4 program using the tooling described in the next Chapter.

The two leftmost examples exist today, and represent the canonical layers for programmable and fixed-function ASICs, respectively. The middle example is purely hypothetical, but it illustrates that it is possible to define a P4-based stack even for a fixed-function pipeline (and by implication, control it using P4Runtime). The fourth example also exists today, and is how Broadcom ASICs conform to the SAI-defined logical pipeline. Finally, the rightmost example projects into the future, when SAI is extended to support P4 programmability and runs on multiple ASICs.

Figure 24: Five example Pipeline/SDK/ASIC stacks. The two leftmost stacks, plus the fourth stack, exist today; the middle stack is hypothetical; and the rightmost stack is a work-in-progress.

Chapter 5: Switch OS

This chapter describes the operating system running on every bare-metal switch. A good mental model is to think of this as analogous to a server OS: there is a general-purpose processor running a Linux-based OS, plus a "packet forwarding accelerator" similar in spirit to a GPU.

The most common foundation for this Switch OS is *Open Network Linux (ONL)*, an open source project of the Open Compute Project. ONL starts with the Debian distribution of Linux, and augments it with support for hardware that is unique to switches, including the *Small Form-factor Pluggable (SFP)* interface module shown in Figure 16.

This chapter does not go into these low-level device driver details, but instead focuses on the *Northbound Interface (NBI)* exported by the Switch OS to the control plane, whether that control plane runs on-switch (as a program running in user space on top of the Switch OS) or off-switch (as an SDN controller like ONOS). And as introduced in Chapter 3, we will use Stratum as our concrete example of the layer of software that implements this NBI on top of ONL. Stratum is sometimes called a *Thin Switch OS*, where the operative word is "thin" because it essentially implements an API shim. What's interesting about the shim is the set of APIs it supports, and correspondingly, the vast majority of this chapter focuses on those APIs.

5.1 Thin Switch OS

This section describes the set of components that implement an SDN-ready Northbound Interface for the Switch OS running on a bare-metal switch. The details are drawn from Stratum, an open source project at the ONF that started with production-quality code made available by Google. Figure 25 gives a high-level overview of Stratum, and to re-emphasize, it's the exposed interfaces—P4Runtime, gNMI, and gNOI—that are the important take-aways of this chapter. We show these few implementation details in this section only as a way of grounding the description of an end-to-end workflow for developers implementing SDN-based solutions.

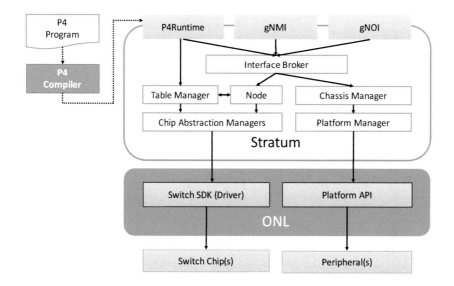

Figure 25: High-level schematic of Stratum, a Thin Switch OS running on top of Open Networking Linux.

Stratum exports three primary Northbound Interfaces: (1) P4Runtime is used to control the switch's forwarding behavior; (2) gNMI is used to configure the switch; and (3) gNOI is used to access other operational variables on the switch. All three interfaces are gRPC services (not shown), which implies there is a corresponding set of *Protocol Buffers (protobufs)* that specify the API methods and supported parameters of each. A tutorial on gRPC and protobufs is beyond the scope of this book, but a brief introduction to both can be found online.

The important take-away is that by using protobufs and gRPC, Stratum need not be concerned with the long list of formatting, reliability, backwards compatibility, and security challenges that protocols (including OpenFlow) have historically spent a great deal of time

Further Reading:
gRPC. *Computer Networks: A Systems Approach,* 2020.

Protocol Buffers. *Computer Networks: A Systems Approach,* 2020.

worrying about. In addition, protobufs serve as a well-defined target for the code generated by the P4 compiler, which is to say, the P4 toolchain outputs protobufs that specify the types and arguments for the P4Runtime interface. This API, along with the client- and server-side stubs that implement it, are (mostly) auto-generated. Section 5.2 describes the toolchain for creating this runtime contract in more detail.

Below Stratum, the architecture takes advantage of two components. The first is a *Software Development Kit (SDK)* for the on-board switching chip(s). These are provided by the switch vendor, and in the case of Broadcom, it roughly corresponds to the OF-DPA layer described in Section 4.5. Barefoot provides a similar SDK for their Tofino chip. You can think of these SDKs as similar to device drivers in a traditional OS: they are used to indirectly read and write memory locations on the corresponding chip. The second is the *ONL Platform (ONLP)*, which exports the Platform API shown in Figure 25. This API provides access to hardware counters, monitors, status variables, and so on.

As a simple example, which helps illustrate the fundamental difference between fixed-function and programmable pipelines, Broadcom's SDK defines a bcm_l3_route_create method to update the L3 forwarding table, whereas Barefoot's corresponding pipeline-independent method is bf_table_write.

Internal to Stratum, the rest of the components shown in Figure 25 are primarily designed to make Stratum vendor-agnostic. In the case of a programmable chip like Tofino, Stratum is largely pass-through: P4Runtime calls that come from above are directly passed through to the Barefoot SDK. In the case of a fixed-function chip like Tomahawk, Stratum maintains the runtime state it needs to translate the P4Runtime calls into their Broadcom SDK counterpart. To a first approximation, this implies mapping P4Runtime calls switch.p4 (Section 4.5.1) into Broadcom SDK calls. For example, a P4Runtime call to update table entries in a program like switch.p4 (Section 4.5.1) would be mapped into a Broadcom SDK call to update entries in one of the ASIC tables.

5.2 P4Runtime

You can think of the P4Runtime interface shown in Figure 25 as the server-side RPC stub for controlling the switch. There is a corresponding client-side stub, which is similarly included in the SDN Controller. Together, they implement the *P4Runtime Contract* between the controller and the switch. The toolchain for generating this contract is shown in Figure 26, where as in earlier figures, we represent the original P4 forwarding program as an abstract graph rather than with actual P4 source code.

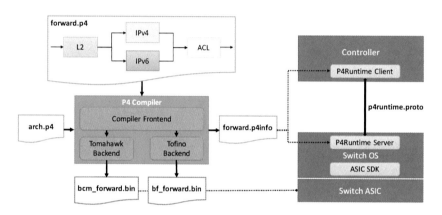

Figure 26: P4 toolchain achieves ASIC-independence and auto-generates P4Runtime Contract (represented as a Protocol Buffer specification).

One key takeaway from Figure 26 is that the P4 compiler generates both the binary that is loaded into each switching chip, and the *runtime interface* used to control the switching chip (indirectly via the Switch OS).[14] The compiler does this with the help of a vendor-specific backend, where Figure 26 shows two possible examples. Note that these vendor-specific backends have to be written for a specific architecture model (as defined by arch.p4 in this example). In other words, today it is a combination of the P4 language, the ASIC-specific backend, and the architecture model that defines the programming environment for injecting functionality into the data plane.

The final piece of the end-to-end story is the connection between the runtime contract and the original program loaded into the data plane. Using the simple forwarding program presented in Section 4.4 as an example, we see that forward.p4 defines a lookup table:

[14] When we say the binary is loaded into the switching chip, we are adopting familiar terminology from general-purpose processors. The exact process is ASIC-specific, and might include initializing various on-chip tables via the SDK.

```
table ipv4_lpm {
    key = {
        hdr.ipv4.dstAddr: lpm;
    }
    actions = {
        ipv4_forward;
        drop;
        NoAction;
    }
    size = 1024;
    default_action = drop();
}
```

Correspondingly, the file forward.p4info output by the compiler *specifies* the P4Runtime Contract. As shown in the following example, it contains enough information to fully inform both the controller and switch on how to format and interpret the set of gRPC methods needed to insert, read, modify, and delete entries in this table. For example, the table definition identifies the field to match (hdr.ipv4.dstAddr) and the type of match (LPM), along with the three possible actions.

```
actions {
    preamble {
        id: 16800567
        name: "NoAction"
        alias: "NoAction"
    }
}
actions {
    preamble {
        id: 16805608
        name: "MyIngress.drop"
        alias: "drop"
    }
}
actions {
    preamble {
        id: 16799317
        name: "MyIngress.ipv4_forward"
        alias: "ipv4_forward"
```

```
        }
    params {
        id: 1
        name: "dstAddr"
        bitwidth: 48
    }
    params {
        id: 2
        name: "port"
        bitwidth: 9
    }
}
tables {
    preamble {
        id: 33574068
        name: "MyIngress.ipv4_lpm"
        alias: "ipv4_lpm"
    }
    match_fields {
        id: 1
        name: "hdr.ipv4.dstAddr"
        bitwidth: 32
        match_type: LPM
    }
    action_refs {
        id: 16799317
    }
    action_refs {
        id: 16805608
    }
    action_refs {
        id: 16800567
    }
    size: 1024
}
```

The gRPC toolchain takes over from there. For this to work, the toolchain must be aware of which P4 language elements are controllable, and hence, available to be "exposed" by p4runtime.proto. Such information is contained in forward.p4info, which specifies exactly the set of controllable elements and their attributes as defined in the source

P4 program.[15] The table element is one obvious example, but there are others, including counters and meters, which are used to report status information up to the controller and to allow the controller to specify a QoS rate, respectively, but neither are included in our example program.

Finally, a controller actually writes an entry to this table. While in general this controller would run on top of ONOS, and so indirectly interact with the switch, we can look at a simpler example in which a Python program implements the controller, and writes an entry directly into the table (assisted by a P4Runtime library).

```
import p4runtime_lib.helper

        ...
table_entry = p4info_helper.buildTableEntry(
    table_name="MyIngress.ipv4_lpm",
    match_fields={
        "hdr.ipv4.dstAddr": (dst_ip_addr, 32)
    },
    action_name="MyIngress.ipv4_forward",
    action_params={
        "dstAddr": next_hop_mac_addr,
        "port": outport,
    })
ingress_sw.WriteTableEntry(table_entry)
```

5.3 gNMI and gNOI

A core challenge of configuring and operating any network device is to define the set of variables available for operators to GET and SET on the device, with the additional requirement that this dictionary of variables be uniform across devices (i.e., be vendor-agnostic). The Internet has already gone through one decades-long exercise defining such a dictionary, resulting in the *Management Information Base (MIB)* used in conjunction with SNMP. But the MIB was more focused on *reading* device status variables than *writing* device configuration variables, where the latter has historically been done using the device's *Command Line Interface (CLI)*. One consequence of the SDN transfor-

[15] In principle, this P4Info file is not strictly required, as the controller and switch could use the source P4 program to derive all the information they need to handle P4Runtime methods. However, P4Info makes that much easier by extracting the relevant information from the P4 program and providing them in a more structured protobuf-defined format, which is straightforward to parse by using a protobuf library.

mation is to nudge the industry towards support for programmatic configuration APIs. This means revisiting the information model for network devices.

The main technical advance that was not prevalent in the early days of SNMP and MIB is the availability of pragmatic modeling languages, where YANG is the leading choice to have emerged over the last few years. YANG—which stands for *Yet Another Next Generation*, a name chosen to poke fun at how often a do-over proves necessary—can be viewed as a restricted version of XSD, which is a language for defining a schema for XML. YANG defines the structure of the data, but unlike XSD, it is not XML-specific. Instead, YANG can be used in conjunction with different over-the-wire message formats, including XML, but also protobufs and JSON. If these acronyms are unfamiliar, or the distinction between a markup language and a schema for a markup language is fuzzy, a gentle introduction is available online.

What's important about going in this direction is that the data model that defines the semantics of the variables available to be read and written is available in a programmatic form; it's not just text in a standards document. Moreover, while it is true that all hardware vendors promote the unique capabilities of their products, it is not a free-for-all with each vendor defining a unique model. This is because the network operators that buy network hardware have a strong incentive to drive the models for similar devices towards convergence, and vendors have an equally strong incentive to adhere to those models. YANG makes the process of creating, using, and modifying models programmable, and hence, adaptable to this iterative process.

This is where an industry-wide standardization effort, called *OpenConfig*, comes into play. OpenConfig is a group of network operators trying to drive the industry towards a common set of configuration models using YANG as its modeling language. OpenConfig is officially agnostic as to the over-the-wire protocol used to access on-device configuration and status variables, but gNMI (gRPC Network Management Interface) is one approach it is actively pursuing. And as you might guess from its name, gNMI uses gRPC (which in turn runs on top of HTTP/2). This means gNMI also adopts protobufs as the

Further Reading:
Markup Languages (XML). *Computer Networks: A Systems Approach*, 2020.

way it specifies the data actually communicated over the HTTP connection. Thus, gNMI is intended as a standard management interface for network devices.

For completeness, note that NETCONF is another of the post-SNMP protocols for communicating configuration information to network devices. OpenConfig also works with NETCONF, but our current assessment is that gNMI has the weight of industry behind it as the future management protocol. For this reason, it is the one we highlight in our description of the full SDN software stack.

OpenConfig defines a hierarchy of object types. For example, the YANG model for network interfaces looks like this:

```
Module: openconfig-interfaces
      +--rw interfaces
            +--rw interface*   [name]
                  +--rw name
                  +--rw config
                  |   ...
                  +--ro state
                  |   ...
                  +--rw hold-time
                  |   ...
                  +--rw subinterfaces
                        |   ...
```

This is a base model that can be augmented, for example, to model an Ethernet interface:

```
Module: openconfig-if-ethernet
      augment /ocif:interfaces/ocif:interface:
            +--rw ethernet
            +--rw config
            |        +--rw mac-address?
            |        +--rw auto-negotiate?
            |        +--rw duplex-mode?
            |        +--rw port-speed?
            |        +--rw enable-flow-control?
            +--ro state
                  +--ro mac-address?
```

```
                    +--ro auto-negotiate?
                    +--ro duplex-mode?
                    +--ro port-speed?
                    +--ro enable-flow-control?
                    +--ro hw-mac-address?
                    +--ro counters
                              ...
```

Other similar augmentations might be defined to support link aggregation, IP address assignment, VLAN tags, and so on.

Each model in the OpenConfig hierarchy defines a combination of configuration state that can be both read and written by the client (denoted rw in the examples), and operational state that reports device status (denoted ro in the examples, indicating it is read-only from the client side). This distinction between declarative configuration state and runtime feedback state is a fundamental aspect of any network device interface, where OpenConfig is explicitly focused on generalizing the latter to include network telemetry data the operator needs to track.

Cloud Best Practices

Our commentary on OpenConfig vs NETCONF is grounded in a fundamental tenet of SDN, which is about bringing best practices in cloud computing to the network. It involves big ideas like implementing the network control plane as a scalable cloud service, but it also includes more narrow benefits, such as using modern messaging frameworks like gRPC and protobufs.

The advantages in this particular case are tangible: (1) improved and optimized transport using HTTP/2 and protobuf-based marshalling instead of SSH plus hand-coded marshalling; (2) binary data encodings instead of text-based encoding; (3) diff-oriented data exchange instead of snapshot-based responses; and (4) native support for server push and client streaming.

Having a meaningful set of models is necessary, but a full configuration system includes other elements as well. In our case, there are three important points to make about the relationship between Stratum and the OpenConfig models.

The first is that Stratum depends on a YANG toolchain. Figure 27 shows the steps involved in translating a set of YANG-based OpenConfig models into the client-side and server-side gRPC stubs used by gNMI. The gNMI Server shown in the figure is the same as the gNMI interface portal shown in Figure 25. The toolchain supports multiple target programming languages (Stratum happens to use C++), where the client and server sides of the gRPC need not be written in the same language.

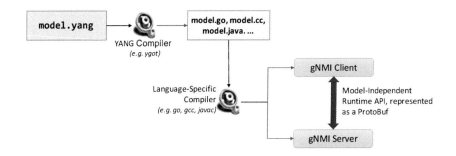

Figure 27: YANG toolchain used to generate gRPC-based runtime for gNMI.

Keep in mind that YANG is not tied to either gRPC or gNMI. The toolchain is able to start with the very same OpenConfig models, but instead produce XML or JSON representations for the data being read-from or written-to network devices using (for example) NETCONF or RESTCONF, respectively. But in our context, the target is protobufs, which Stratum uses to support gNMI running over gRPC.

The second point is that gNMI defines a specific set of gRPC methods to operate on these models. The set is defined collectively as a Service in the protobuf specification:

```
Service gNMI {
    rpc Capabilities(CapabilityRequest)
        returns (CapabilityResponse);
    rpc Get(GetRequest) returns (GetResponse);
    rpc Set(SetRequest) returns (SetResponse);
    rpc Subscribe(stream SubscribeRequest)
        returns (stream SubscribeResponse);
}
```

The Capabilities method is used to retrieve the set of model definitions supported by the device. The Get and Set methods are used to read and write the corresponding variable defined in some model. The Subscribe method is used to set up a stream of telemetry updates from the device. The corresponding arguments and return values (e.g., GetRequest, GetResponse) are defined by a defined by a protobuf Message, and include various fields from the YANG models. A given field is specified by giving its fully qualified path name in the data model tree.

The third point is that Stratum does not necessarily care about the full range of OpenConfig models. This is because—as a Switch OS designed to support a centralized Controller—Stratum cares about configuring various aspects of the data plane, but is not typically involved in configuring control plane protocols like BGP. Such control plane protocols are no longer implemented on the switch in an SDN-based solution (although they remain in scope for the Network OS, which implements their centralized counterpart). To be specific, Stratum tracks the following OpenConfig models: Interfaces, VLANs, QoS, and LACP (link aggregation), in addition to a set of system and platform variables (of which the switch's fan speed is everyone's favorite example).

We conclude this section by briefly turning our attention to gNOI, but there isn't a lot to say. This is because the underlying mechanism used by gNOI is exactly the same as for gNMI, and in the larger scheme of things, there is little difference between a switch's configuration interface and its operations interface. Generally speaking, persistent state is handled by gNMI (and a corresponding YANG model is defined), whereas clearing or setting ephemeral state is handled by gNOI. It is also the case that non-idempotent actions like reboot and ping tend to fall under gNOI's domain. In any case, the two are closely enough aligned to collectively be referred to as gNXI.

As an illustrative example of what gNOI is used for, the following is the protobuf specification for the System service:

```
service System {
    rpc Ping(PingRequest)
        returns (stream PingResponse) {}
    rpc Traceroute(TracerouteRequest)
        returns (stream TracerouteResponse) {}
    rpc Time(TimeRequest)
        returns (TimeResponse) {}
    rpc SetPackage(stream SetPackageRequest)
        returns (SetPackageResponse) {}
    rpc Reboot(RebootRequest)
        returns (RebootResponse) {}
    // ...
}
```

where, for example, the following protobuf message defines the RebootRequest parameter:

```
message RebootRequest {
    // COLD, POWERDOWN, HALT, WARM, NSF, ...
    RebootMethod method = 1;
    // Delay in nanoseconds before issuing reboot.
    uint64 delay = 2;
    // Informational reason for the reboot.
    string message = 3;
    // Optional sub-components to reboot.
    repeated types.Path subcomponents = 4;
    // Force reboot if sanity checks fail.
    bool force = 5;
}
```

Further Reading:
Protocol Buffers. *Computer Networks: A Systems Approach*, 2020.

As a reminder, if you are unfamiliar with protobufs, a brief overview is available online.

5.4 SONiC

In the same way SAI is an industry-wide switch abstraction (see Section 4.5), SONiC is a vendor-agnostic Switch OS that is gaining a lot of momentum in the industry. SONiC, which leverages SAI as a vendor-agnostic SDK and was originally open sourced by Microsoft, continues to serve as the Switch OS for the Azure Cloud. And like Stratum, SONiC can also leverage Open Networking Linux (ONL) as its underlying operating system. All of which is to say that Stratum and SONiC both try to fill the same need. Today their respective approaches are largely complementary, with both open source communities working towards a "best of both worlds" solution.

Both SONiC and Stratum support a configuration interface, so unifying those will be a matter of reconciling their respective data models and toolchains. The main distinction is Stratum's support for programmable forwarding pipelines (including both P4 and P4Runtime), versus the least common denominator approach to forwarding taken by SAI. Developers on the two open source projects are working together to define a roadmap that will make it possible for interested networks to take advantage of programmable pipelines in an incremental and low-risk way.

The goal of this effort is both (1) to enable remote SDN Controllers/Apps to interact with SAI using P4Runtime and gNMI, and (2) to enable SAI extensions using P4 so as to improve feature velocity in the data plane. Both goals rely on a new representation of the SAI behavioral model and pipeline based on a P4 program (the so called sai.p4 program shown in Figure 24 of Section 4.6). If you take one thing away from this reconciliation effort, it should be that embracing a programmable pipeline (and corresponding toolchain) is what facilitates doing something like this.

Chapter 6: Network OS

We are now ready to move from a single switch with purely local state, to the global, network-wide view maintained by a Network Operating System. The best way to think about a NOS is that it is like any other horizontally scalable cloud application. It consists of a collection of loosely coupled subsystems—as is often associated with a micro-service architecture—including a scalable and highly available key/value store.

This chapter describes the overall structure of a NOS using ONOS as a reference implementation. The focus is on the core abstractions that have emerged from experience implementing a wide range of control applications on top of ONOS, and using ONOS to manage an equally wide range of network devices. This chapter also discusses the critically important issues of scalable performance and high availability.

6.1 ONOS Architecture

The overall architecture for ONOS is shown in Figure 28. It consists of three main layers:

1. A collection of Northbound Interfaces (NBI) that applications use to stay informed about the network state (e.g. traverse topology graph, intercept network packets) and also to control the network data plane (e.g. program flow objectives via FlowObjective API introduced in Chapter 3).

2. A Distributed Core that is responsible for managing network state

and notifying applications about relevant changes in that state. Internal to the core is a scalable key/value store called Atomix.

3. A Southbound Interface (SBI) constructed from a collection of plugins including shared protocol libraries and device-specific drivers.

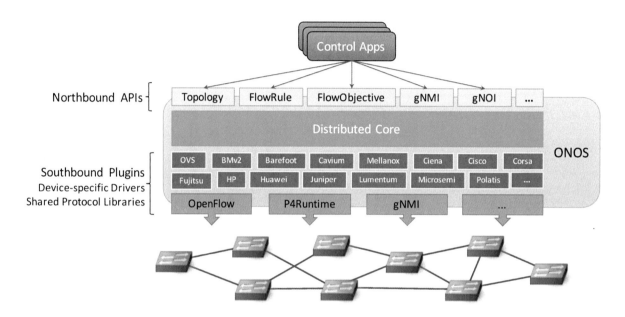

As Figure 28 suggests, the design is highly modular, with a given deployment configured to include the subset of modules it requires. We delay a discussion about the exact form for the modularity (e.g., Karaf, Kubernetes) until the concluding section, where we take up the issue of scalability. Until then, the focus is on the functional organization of ONOS.

There are three other things to note about Figure 28 before we get into the details about each layer. The first is the breadth of the NBI. If you think of ONOS as an operating system, this makes sense: All access to the underlying hardware, whether by a control program or a human operator, is mediated by ONOS. This means the union of all northbound APIs must be sufficient to configure, operate, and control the network. For example, the NBI includes gNMI and gNOI for con-

Figure 28: Three-layer architecture of ONOS, hosting a set of control applications.

figuration and operations, respectively. It also means the NBI includes a Topology API that Control Applications use to learn about changes in the underlying network state (e.g., ports coming up and down), along with the FlowObjective API used to control the underlying switches.

As an aside, while we generally characterize the applications that run on top of a Network OS as implementing the network control plane, there are actually a wide assortment of apps running on ONOS, implementing everything from a GUI that can be used to monitor the state of the network, to a traditional CLI that operators can use to issue directives.

Among the applications sitting on top of ONOS is a zero-touch management plane that provisions new hardware added to the network, making sure the right software, certificates, configuration parameters, and pipeline definition are installed. This example is illustrated in Figure 29, where one takeaway is that ONOS does not have a fixed NBI: there are potentially multiple layers of applications and services running on ONOS, each providing some value on top of the applications and services below it. Declaring zero-touch provisioning to be *in* ONOS versus *on* ONOS is an arbitrary statement, which points to an important way in which ONOS is *not* like a conventional operating system: There is no syscall-equivalent interface demarking the boundary between a privileged kernel and multiple user domains. In other words, ONOS currently operates in a single trust domain.

The second thing to note about Figure 28 is that ONOS maps an abstract specification of behavior the control application wants to impose on the network onto the concrete instructions that need to be communicated to each switch in the network. Applications can select from a variety of means to affect the network operation. Some applications use high-level *Intents*, which are network-wide, topology-independent programming constructs. Others that require finer-grained control use Flow Objectives, which are device-centric programming constructs. Flow Objectives are much like Flow Rules, except they are pipeline-independent. Applications use them to control both fixed-function and programmable pipelines. As highlighted in Figure 30, doing this

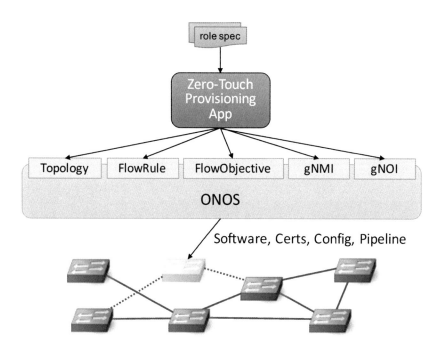

Figure 29: Example of a Zero-Touch Provisioning (ZTP) application taking a "role spec" for a switch being installed as input, with ONOS provisioning the switch accordingly.

job in the face of varied forwarding pipelines is a complexity ONOS is explicitly designed to address.

The third thing to notice about Figure 28 is that information flows both "down" and "up" through ONOS. It's easy to focus on applications using the ONOS NBI to control the network, but it is also the case that the southbound plugins pass information about the underlying network up to the ONOS core. This includes intercepting packets, discovering devices and their ports, reporting link quality, and so on. These interactions between the ONOS core and the network devices are handled by a set of adaptors (e.g., OpenFlow, P4Runtime), which hide the details of communicating with the devices, thereby insulating the ONOS core and the applications running on top of it from the diversity of network devices. For example, ONOS is being used to control proprietary switches, bare-metal switches, optical devices, and cellular base stations.

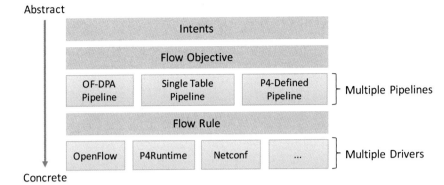

Figure 30: ONOS manages the mapping of an abstract specification of network-wide behavior to a collection of per-device instructions.

6.2 Distributed Core

The ONOS core is comprised of a number of subsystems, each responsible for a particular aspect of network state (e.g. topology, host tracking, packet intercept, flow programming). Each subsystem maintains its own *service abstraction*, where its implementation is responsible for propagating the state throughout the cluster.

Many ONOS services are built using distributed tables (maps), which are in turn implemented using a distributed key/value store. The store will be familiar to anyone who has looked at how modern cloud services are designed—it scales across a distributed set of servers, and implements a consensus algorithm to achieve fault-tolerance in the event of failures. The specific algorithm used in ONOS is Raft, which is well described in a paper by Diego Ongaro and John Ousterhout. The web site also provides a helpful visualization tool.

ONOS uses Atomix as its store. Atomix goes beyond the core Raft algorithm to provide a rich set of programming primitives that ONOS uses to manage the distributed state and to provide easy access to that state by the control apps.

This approach is a common design paradigm, which results in a system that is both scalable (runs on enough virtualized instances to handle the request workload) and highly available (run on enough instances to continue offering service in the face of failure). What's

Further Reading:
D. Ongaro and J. Ousterhout. The Raft Consensus Algorithm.

specific to ONOS—or any Network OS, for that matter—is the set of maps it defines: the semantics of the keys it stores and the types of the values associated with those keys. It is this data model that makes a Network OS a Network OS (and not, say, a ride-share application or a social network). This section mostly focuses on this set of data models and the corresponding services built around them, although we start with a brief introduction to the primitives that Atomix supports.

6.2.1 Atomix Primitives

The preceding discussion introduced Atomix as a key/value store, which it is, but it is also accurate to describe Atomix as a general tool for building distributed systems. It is a Java-based system that includes support for:

- Distributed data structures, including maps, sets, trees, and counters.

- Distributed communication, including direct messaging and publish/subscribe.

- Distributed coordination, including locks, leader elections, and barriers.

- Managing group membership.

For example, Atomix includes AtomicMap and DistributedMap primitives. Both extend Java's Map utility with additional methods. In the case of AtomicMap, the primitive performs atomic updates using optimistic locks, such that all operations are guaranteed to be atomic (and each value in a map has a monotonically increasing version number). In contrast, the DistributedMap primitive supports eventual consistency rather than guaranteed consistency. Both primitives support event-based notifications of changes to the corresponding map. Clients can listen for inserted/updated/removed entries by registering event listeners on a map.

Maps are the workhorse primitive used by ONOS, as we will see in the next subsection. We conclude this section by looking at another role that Atomix plays in ONOS: coordinating all the ONOS instances.[16] There are two aspects to this coordination.

First, as a horizontally scalable service, the number of ONOS instances running at any given time depends on the workload and the level of replication needed to guarantee availability in the face of failures. The Atomix *group membership* primitive is used to determine the set of available instances, making it possible to detect new instances that have been spun up and existing instances that have failed. (Note that the set of ONOS instances are distinct from the set of Atomix instances, with both able to scale independently. This and the next paragraph are focused on the ONOS instances.)

Second, the primary job of each instance is to monitor and control a subset of the physical switches in the network. The approach ONOS takes is to elect a master instance for each switch, where only the master issues (writes) control instructions to a given switch. All the instances are able to monitor (read) switch state. The instances then use the Atomix *leader-election* primitive to determine the master for each switch. Should an ONOS instance fail, the same primitive is used to elect a new master for the switches. The same approach is applied when a new switch comes on-line.

6.2.2 Services

ONOS builds on Atomix by defining a core set of tables (maps), which are in turn packaged as a collection of *services* available to control applications (and other services). A table and a service are two ways of looking at the same things: one is a collection of key/value pairs and the other is the interface through which applications and other services interact with those pairs. Figure 31 depicts the respective layers, where the middle three components—Topology, Link, and Device—are example ONOS services.

Note that the Topology Service in Figure 31 does not have an associated map, but instead indirectly accesses the maps defined by the Link and Device Services. The Topology Service caches the resulting network graph in memory, which gives applications a low-latency, read-only way to access network state. The Topology Service also

[16] For the purpose of this discussion, assume ONOS is packaged as a whole, and then scaled across multiple virtualized instances. An alternative partitioning of ONOS functionality into independently scaled microservices is discussed in Section 6.5.

110

computes a spanning tree of the graph to ensure that all applications see the same broadcast tree.

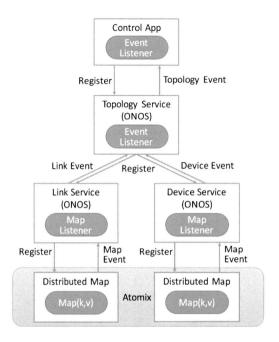

Figure 31: ONOS provides a set of services, such as the Topology, Device, and Link Services, on top of a corresponding table (Map) implemented in Atomix.

As a whole, ONOS defines an inter-connected graph of services, with Figure 31 showing just a small subgraph. Figure 32 expands on that view to illustrate some other aspects of the ONOS core, this time simplified to show the Atomix maps as an attribute of some (but not all) of the services.

There are several things of note about this dependency graph. First, the Path Service, which applications can query to learn end-to-end paths between host pairs, depends on both the Topology Service (which tracks the network graph) and a Host Service (which tracks the hosts connected to the network). Note that arrow directionality implies dependency, but as we see in Figure 32, information flows in both directions.

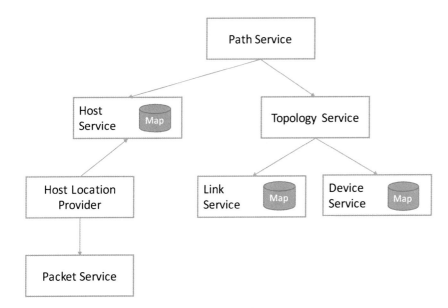

Figure 32: Dependency graph of services (some with their own key/value maps) involved in building a Path Service.

Second, the Host Service has both a north-bound and a south-bound interface. The Path Service uses its north-bound interface to read host-related information, while the Host Location Provider uses its south-bound interface to write host-related information. The Host Service itself is little more than a wrapper around the Atomix Map that stores information about hosts. We return to the *Provider* abstraction in Section 6.4, but, in a nutshell, they are modules that interact with the underlying network devices.

Third, the Host Location Provider snoops network traffic—for example, intercepting ARP, NDP, and DHCP packets—to learn about hosts connected to the network, which it then provides to the Host Service. The Host Location Provider, in turn, depends on a Packet Service to help it intercept those packets. The Packet Service defines a device-independent means for other ONOS services to instruct the underlying switches to capture and forward select packets to the control plane. ONOS services can also use the Packet Service to inject packets into the data plane.

Finally, while the service graph depicted in Figure 32 is designed to discover the network topology, there are many scenarios where the topology is fixed, and known *a priori*. This often happens when the control plane is tailored for a particular topology, as is the case for the leaf-spine topology discussed throughout this book. For such scenarios, the Topology Service accepts configuration instructions from a control application (or high-level service) sitting above it in the dependency graph.[17] ONOS includes such a configuration service, called *Network Config*, as depicted in Figure 33. Network Config, in turn, accepts configuration directives from either a human operator or an automated orchestrator, such as the example ZTP control application from Figure 29.

[17] The Topology Service still collects ground-truth information from the underlying network, verifies that it matches the configuration directives passed in from above, and notifies the Network Config Service when there is a discrepancy.

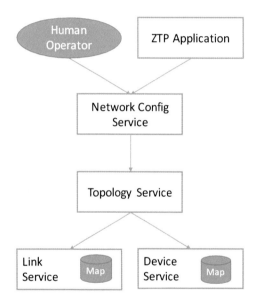

Figure 33: Network Config Service, supporting both provisioning applications and human operators.

   The sequence of examples we just walked through (Figures 31, 32, and 33) illustrates the basics of how ONOS is built from parts. For completeness, the following gives a summary of the most commonly used ONOS services:

  Host: Records end systems (machine or virtual machine) connected to the network. Populated by one or more host discovery apps, generally by intercepting ARP, NDP, or DHCP packets.

Device: Records infrastructure device-specific information (switches, ROADMs, etc.), including ports. Populated by one or more device discovery apps.

Link: Records attributes of links connecting pairs of infrastructure devices/ports. Populated by one or more link discovery apps (e.g., by emitting and intercepting LLDP packets).

Topology: Represents the network as a whole using a graph abstraction. It is built on top of the Device and Link services and provides a coherent graph comprised of infrastructure devices as vertices and infrastructure links as edges. The graph converges on the network topology using an eventual consistency approach as events about device and link inventory are received.

Mastership: Runs leadership contests (using the Atomix leader-election primitive) to elect which ONOS instance in the cluster should be the master for each infrastructure device. In cases when an ONOS instance fails (e.g., server power failure), it makes sure a new master is elected as soon as possible for all devices left without one.

Cluster: Manages ONOS cluster configuration. It provides information about the Atomix cluster nodes as well as about all peer ONOS nodes. Atomix nodes form the actual cluster that is the basis for consensus, while the ONOS nodes are effectively mere clients used to scale control logic and I/O to network devices. Entries are set by ONOS using the Atomix membership primitive.

Network Config: Prescribes meta-information about the network, such as devices and their ports, hosts, links, etc. Provides outside information about the network and how the network should be treated by ONOS core and applications. Set by orchestrator apps, the ZTP control application, or manually by an operator.

Component Config: Manages configuration parameters for various software components in the ONOS core and applications. Such parameters (i.e. how to treat foreign flow rules, address or DHCP server, polling frequency, and so on) allow for tailoring the behavior of the software. Set by the operator according to the needs of the deployment.

Packet: Allows the core services and applications to intercept packets (packet in) and to emit packets back into the network. This is the basis for most of the host and link discovery methods (e.g., ARP, DHCP, LLDP).

The above services are used by nearly every application because they offer information about the network devices and their topology. There are, however, many more services, including ones that allow applications to program the behavior of the network using different constructs and different levels of abstraction. We discuss some of these in more depth in the next section, but for now we note that they include:

Route: Defines a prefix to nexthop mapping. Set either by a control app or manually configured by an operator.

Mcast: Defines group IP, source and sink locations. Set by a control app or manually configured by an operator.

Group: Aggregates ports or actions in a device. Flow entries can point to a defined group to allow sophisticated means of forwarding, such as load-balancing between ports in a group, failover among ports in a group, or multicast to all ports specified in a group. A group can also be used for aggregating common actions of different flows, so that in some scenarios only one group entry is required to be modified for all the referencing flow entries instead of having to modify all of them.

Meter: Expresses a rate-limit to enforce a quality of service for select network traffic handled by a device.

Flow Rule: Provides a device-centric, match/action pair for programming the data-plane forwarding behavior of a device. It requires that flow rule entries be composed in accordance with the device's table pipeline structure and capabilities.

Flow Objective: Provides a device-centric abstraction for programming the forwarding behavior of a device in a pipeline-agnostic manner. It relies on the Pipeliner subsystem (see next section) to implement the mapping between table-agnostic flow objectives and table-specific flow rules or groups.

Intent: Provides a topology-agnostic way to establish flows across the network. High-level specifications, call *intents*, indicate various hints and constraints for the end-to-end path, including the type of traffic and the source and destination hosts, or ingress and egress ports to request connectivity. The service provisions this connectivity over the appropriate paths and then continuously monitors the network, changing the paths over time to continue meeting the objectives prescribed by the intent in the face of varying network conditions.

Each of the above services comprises its own distributed store and notification capabilities. Individual applications are free to extend this set with their own services and to back their implementations with their own distributed stores. This is why ONOS provides applications with direct access to Atomix primitives, such as AtomicMaps and DistributedMaps. We will see examples of such extensions in the next Chapter when we take a closer look at Trellis.

6.3 Northbound Interface

The ONOS NBI has multiple parts. First, for every service included in a given configuration of ONOS, there is a corresponding API. For example, the "Topology" interface shown in Figure 28 is exactly the API offered by the Topology Service shown in Figure 31. Second, because ONOS permits applications to define and use their own Atomix tables, it is fair to consider the Atomix programmatic interface as another part of the ONOS NBI. Third, the ONOS NBI includes gNMI and gNOI. These are standardized interfaces, defined independent of ONOS, but supported as part of the ONOS NBI. Note that the implementation sitting behind gNMI and gNOI are also ONOS services wrapped around Atomix maps. Finally, and most interestingly, ONOS offers a set of interfaces for controlling the underlying switches. Figure 28 depicts two: Flow Rules and Flow Objectives. The first is borrowed from OpenFlow, and hence, is pipeline-aware. The second is pipeline-agnostic, and the focus of the rest of this section.

There are three types of flow objectives: *Filtering*, *Forwarding*, and *Next*. Filtering objectives determine whether or not traffic should be permitted to enter the pipeline, based on a traffic *Selector*. Forwarding objectives determine what traffic is to be allowed to egress the pipeline, generally by matching select fields in the packet with a forwarding table. Next objectives indicate what kind of *Treatment* the traffic should receive, such as how the header is to be rewritten. If this sounds like an abstract three-stage pipeline:

$$\text{Filtering} \rightarrow \text{Forwarding} \rightarrow \text{Next}$$

then you understand the idea behind Flow Objectives. For example, the Filter objective (stage) might specify that packets matching a particular MAC address, VLAN tag, and IP address be allowed to enter the pipeline; the corresponding Forwarding objective (stage) then looks up the IP address in a routing table; and finally the Next objective (stage) rewrites the headers as necessary and assigns the packet to an output port. All three stages, of course, are agnostic as to exactly what combination of tables in the underlying switch are used to implement the corresponding sequence of match/action pairs.

The challenge is to map these pipeline-agnostic objectives onto the corresponding pipeline-dependent rules. In ONOS, this mapping is managed by the Flow Objective Service, as depicted in Figure 34. For simplicity, the example focuses on the selector (match) specified by a Filtering objective, where the key is to express the fact that you want to select a particular input port, MAC address, VLAN tag, and IP address combination, without regard for the exact sequence of pipeline tables that implement that combination.

Internally, the Flow Objective Service is organized as a collection of device-specific handlers, each of which is implemented using the ONOS device driver mechanism. The device driver behavior that abstracts the implementation of how flow objective directives should map to flow rule operations is called a *Pipeliner*.

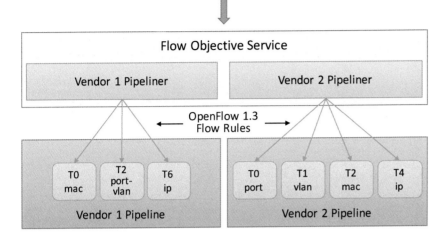

Figure 34: Flow Objective Service manages the mapping of pipeline-agnostic objectives onto pipeline-specific rules.

Pipeliners are able to map flow objectives onto both flow rules (in the case of fixed-function pipelines) and P4-programmed pipelines. The example given in Figure 34 shows the former case, which includes a mapping to OpenFlow 1.3. In the latter case, Pipeliner leverages *Pipeconf*, a structure that maintains associations among the following elements:

1. A model of the pipeline for each target switch.

2. A target-specific driver needed to to deploy flow instructions to the switch.

3. A pipeline-specific translator to map flow objectives into the target pipeline.

Pipeconf maintains these bindings using information extracted from the .p4info file output by the P4 compiler, as described in Section 5.2.

Today, the "model" identified in (1) is ONOS-defined, meaning the end-to-end workflow for a developer involves being aware of both a P4 architecture model (e.g., v1model.p4) when programming the data plane and this ONOS model when programming the control plane using flow objectives. Eventually, these various layers of pipeline models will be unified, and in all likelihood, specified in P4.

```
public void createFlow(
     TrafficSelector originalSelector,
     TrafficTreatment originalTreatment,
     ConnectPoint ingress, ConnectPoint egress,
     int priority, boolean applyTreatment,
     List<Objective> objectives,
     List<DeviceId> devices) {
   TrafficSelector selector = DefaultTrafficSelector.builder(originalSelector)
      .matchInPort(ingress.port())
      .build();

   // Optionally apply the specified treatment
   TrafficTreatment.Builder treatmentBuilder;
   if (applyTreatment) {
      treatmentBuilder = DefaultTrafficTreatment.builder(originalTreatment);
   } else {
      treatmentBuilder =
      DefaultTrafficTreatment.builder();
   }

   objectives.add(DefaultNextObjective.builder()
      .withId(flowObjectiveService.allocateNextId())
      .addTreatment(treatmentBuilder.setOutput(
          egress.port()).build())
      .withType(NextObjective.Type.SIMPLE)
      .fromApp(appId)
      .makePermanent()
      .add());
   devices.add(ingress.deviceId());

   objectives.add(DefaultForwardingObjective.builder()
      .withSelector(selector)
      .nextStep(nextObjective.id())
      .withPriority(priority)
      .fromApp(appId)
      .makePermanent()
      .withFlag(ForwardingObjective.Flag.SPECIFIC)
      .add());
   devices.add(ingress.deviceId());
}
```

Flow objectives are a data structure, packaged with associated constructor routines. A control application builds a list of objectives and passes them to ONOS to be executed. The example code shows flow objectives being constructed to specify an end-to-end flow through the network. The process of applying them to the underlying devices is done elsewhere, and not included in the example.

The example creates a Next objective and a Forwarding objective, with the Next objective applying a Treatment to the flow. Minimally, that Treatment sets the output port, but optionally, it also applies the originalTreatment passed in as an argument to createFlow.

6.4 Southbound Interface

A critical part of ONOS's flexibility is its ability to accommodate different control protocols. While the nature of control interactions and associated abstractions was certainly inspired by the OpenFlow protocol, ONOS is designed to ensure that the core (and the applications written on top of the core) are insulated from the specifics of the control protocol.

This section takes a closer look at how the ONOS accommodates multiple protocols and heterogeneous network devices. The basic approach is based on a plugin architecture, with two types of plugins: *Protocol Providers* and *Device Drivers*. The following subsections describe each, in turn.

6.4.1 Provider Plugins

ONOS defines a Southbound Interface (SBI) plugin framework, where each plugin defines some southbound (network facing) API. Each plugin, called a *Protocol Provider,* serves as a proxy between the SBI and the underlying network, where there is no limitation of what control protocol each can use to communicate with the network. Providers register themselves with the SBI plugin framework, and can start acting as a conduit for passing information and control directives between ONOS applications and core services (above) and the network environment (below), as illustrated in Figure 35.

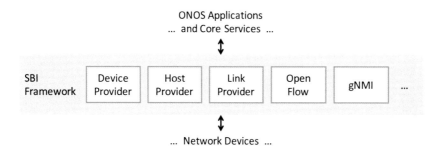

Figure 35: ONOS Southbound Interface (SBI) is extended by Provider Plugins.

Figure 35 includes two general kinds of Provider plugins. The first type are protocol-specific, with OpenFlow and gNMI being typical examples. Each of these Providers effectively bundles the API with the code that implements the corresponding protocol. The second type—of which *DeviceProvider*, *HostProvider*, and *LinkProvider* are the examples shown in the figure—interact indirectly with the environment using some other ONOS service. We saw an example of this in Section 6.2.2, where Host Location Provider (an ONOS service) sits behind *HostProvider* (an SBI plugin); the latter defines the API for host discovery and the former defines one specific approach to discovering hosts (e.g., using Packet Service to intercept ARP, NDP and DHCP packets). Similarly, the LLDP Link Provider Service (corresponding to the *LinkProvider* SBI plugin) uses Packet Service to intercept LLDP and BDDP packets to surmise links between infrastructure devices.

6.4.2 Device Drivers

In addition to insulating the core from protocol specifics, the SBI framework also supports Device Drivers plugins as a mechanism to insulate code (including Providers) from device-specific variations. A Device Driver is a collection of modules, each of which implements a very narrow facet of control or configuration capabilities. As with the Protocol Providers, no limitations are placed on how the device driver chooses to implement those capabilities. Device drivers are also deployed as ONOS applications, which allows them to be installed and uninstalled dynamically, allowing operators to introduce new device types and models on the fly.

6.5 Scalable Performance

ONOS is a logically centralized SDN controller, and as such, must ensure that it is able to respond to a scalable number of control events in a timely way. It must also remain available in the face of failures. This section describes how ONOS scales to meet these performance and availability requirements. We start with some scale and performance numbers, to provide a sense of the state-of-the-art in centralized network control (at the time of writing):

- **Scale:** ONOS supports up to 50 network devices; 5000 network ports; 50k subscribers, 1M routes; and 5M flow rules/groups/meters.

- **Performance:** ONOS supports up to 10k configuration ops/day; 500k flow ops/sec (sustained); 1k topology events/sec (peak); 50ms to detect port/switch up events; 5ms to detect port/switch down events; 3ms for flow ops; and 6ms for hand-over events (RAN).

Production deployments run at least three instances of ONOS, but this is more for availability than performance. Each instance runs on a 32-Core/128GB-RAM server, and is deployed as a Docker container using Kubernetes. Each instance bundles an identical (but configurable) collection of core services, control applications, and protocol providers, and ONOS uses Karaf as its internal modularity framework. The bundle also includes Atomix, although ONOS supports an optional configuration that scales the key/value store independently from the rest of ONOS.

Figure 36 illustrates ONOS scaling across multiple instances, where the set of instances share network state via Atomix Maps. The figure also shows each instance being responsible for a subset of the underlying hardware switches. Should a given instance fail, the remaining instances use the Atomix leader-election primitive to select a new instance to take its place, thereby ensuring high availability.

A refactoring of ONOS to more closely adhere to a microservice architecture is also underway. The new version, called µONOS, leverages ONOS's existing modularity, but packages and scales different subsystems independently. Although in principle each of of the core

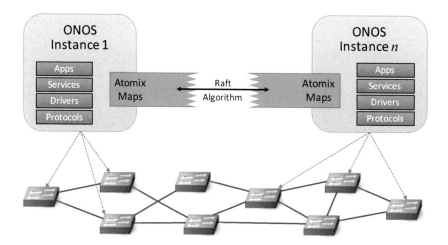

Figure 36: Multiple ONOS instances, all sharing network state via Atomix, provide scalable performance and high availability.

services introduced in this chapter could be packaged as an independent microservice, doing so is much too fine-grain to be practical. Instead, µONOS adopts the following approach. First, it encapsulates Atomix in its own microservice. Second, it runs each control application and southbound adaptor as a separate microservice. Third, it partitions the core into four distinct microservices: (1) a *Topology Management* microservice that exports a Network Graph API; (2) a *Control Management* microservice that exports a P4Runtime API; (3) a *Configuration Management* microservice that exports a gNMI API; and (4) an *Operations Management* microservice that exports a gNOI API.

Chapter 7: Leaf-Spine Fabric

This chapter describes a leaf-spine switching fabric implemented by a collection of control applications. We use Trellis, running on ONOS, as our exemplar implementation. Various aspects of Trellis were introduced in earlier chapters, so we summarize those highlights before getting into the details.

- Trellis supports the leaf-spine fabric topology that is commonly used to interconnect multiple racks of servers in a datacenter (see Figure 9), but it also supports multi-site deployments (see Figure 15). Trellis uses only bare-metal switches, equipped with software described in the previous chapters, to build out the fabric. It can run on a mix of fixed-function and programmable pipelines, but is running in production with the former.

- Trellis supports a wide-range of L2/L3 features, all re-implemented as SDN control apps (with the exception of a DHCP server used to relay DHCP requests and a Quagga BGP server used to exchange BGP routes with external peers). Trellis implements L2 connectivity within each server rack, and L3 connectivity between racks.

- Trellis supports access/edge networking technologies, such as PON (see Figure 11) and RAN (see Figure 15), including support for (a) routing IP traffic to/from devices connected to those access networks, and (b) off-loading access network functionality into the fabric switches.

  This chapter does not give a comprehensive description of all of these features, but it does focus on the datacenter fabric use case, which is sufficient to illustrate the approach to building a production-grade network using SDN principles. More information about the full range of Trellis design decisions is available on the Trellis website.

Further Reading:
Trellis. Open Networking
Foundation, 2020.

7.1 Feature Set

SDN provides an opportunity to customize the network, but for pragmatic reasons, the first requirement for adoption is to reproduce functionality that already exists, and do so in a way that reproduces (or improves upon) the resilience and scalability of legacy solutions. Trellis has satisfied this requirement, which we summarize here.

First, with respect to L2 connectivity, Trellis supports VLANs, including native support for forwarding traffic based on VLAN id, along with QinQ support based on an outer/inner VLAN id pair. Support for QinQ is particularly relevant to access networks, where double tagging is used to isolate traffic belonging to different service classes. In addition, Trellis supports L2 tunnels across the L3 fabric (both single and double tagged).

Second, with respect to L3 connectivity, Trellis supports IPv4 and IPv6 routing for both unicast and multicast addresses. For the latter, Trellis implements centralized multicast tree construction (as opposed to running a protocol like PIM), but does include IGMP support for end hosts wishing to join/leave multicast groups. Trellis also supports both ARP (for IPv4 address translation) and NDP (for IPv6 neighbor discovery), along with support for both DHCPv4 and DHCPv6.

Third, Trellis provides high availability in the face of link or switch failures. It does this through a combination of well-known techniques: dual-homing, link binding, and ECMP link groups. As illustrated in Figure 37, each server in a Trellis cluster is connected to a pair of Top-of-Rack (ToR, or leaf) switches, where the OS running on each compute server implements active-active link bonding. Each leaf switch is then connected by a pair of links to two or more spine switches, with an ECMP group defined for the pair of links connecting each leaf to a given spine and for the set of links connecting each leaf to a set of spines. The cluster as a whole then has multiple connections to external routes, shown via leaf switches 3 and 4 in the Figure. Not shown in Figure 37 is the fact that Trellis runs on top of ONOS, which is itself replicated for the sake of availability. In a configuration like the one shown here, ONOS (and hence the Trellis control applications) are replicated on three to five servers.

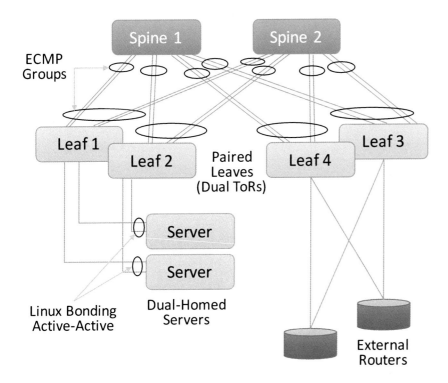

Figure 37: High availability through a combination of dual-homing, link bonding, and ECMP groups.

The use of link aggregation and ECMP is straightforward: the packet forwarding mechanism is augmented to load balance outgoing packets among a group (e.g., a pair) of links (egress ports) rather than having just a single "best" output link (egress port). This both improves bandwidth and results in an automatic recovery mechanism should any single link fail. It is also the case that switch forwarding pipelines have explicit support for port groups, so once equivalences are established, they can be pushed all the way into the data plane.

To be clear, ECMP is a forwarding strategy that Trellis applies uniformly across all the switches in the fabric. The Trellis control application knows the topology, and pushes the port groups into each of the fabric switches accordingly. Each switch then applies these port groups to its forwarding pipeline, which then forwards packets across the set of ports in each group without additional control plane involvement.

Fourth, with respect to scalability, Trellis has demonstrated the ability to support up to 120k routes and 250k flows. This is in a configuration that includes two spine switches and eight leaf switches, the latter implying up to four racks of servers. As with availability, Trellis's ability to scale performance is directly due to ONOS's ability to scale.

7.2 Segment Routing

The previous section focused on *what* Trellis does. This section focuses on *how*. The core strategy in Trellis is based on *Segment Routing (SR)*. The term "segment routing" comes from the idea that the end-to-end path between any pair of hosts can be constructed from a sequence of segments, where label-switching is used to traverse a sequence of segments along an end-to-end path. Segment routing is a general approach to source routing which can be implemented in a number of ways. In the case of Trellis, segment routing leverages the forwarding plane of *Multi-Protocol Label Switching (MPLS)*, which you can read more about online.

When applied to a leaf-spine fabric, there are always two segments involved: leaf-to-spine and spine-to-leaf. Trellis programs the switches to match labeled or unlabeled packets, and to push or pop MPLS labels as needed. Figure 38 illustrates how SR works in Trellis using a simple configuration that forwards traffic between a pair of hosts: 10.0.1.1 and 10.0.2.1. In this example, the servers connected to Leaf 1 are on subnet 10.0.1/24, the servers connected to Leaf 2 are on subnet 10.0.2/24, and each of the switches have an assigned MPLS id: 101, 103, 102, and 104.

Further Reading:
Multi-Protocol Label Switching. *Computer Networks: A Systems Approach,* 2020.

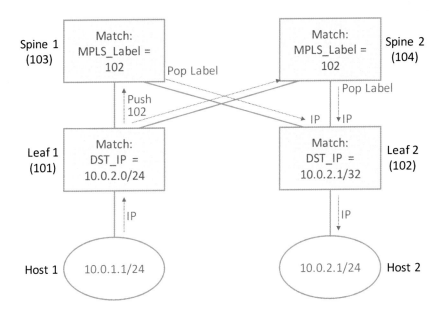

Figure 38: Example of Segment Routing being used to forward traffic between a pair of hosts.

When Host 1 sends a packet with destination address 10.0.2.1 it is by default forwarded to the server's ToR/leaf switch. Leaf 1 matches the destination IP address, learns this packet needs to cross the fabric and emerge at Leaf 2 to reach subnet 10.0.2/24, and so pushes the MPLS label 102 onto the packet. Because of ECMP, Leaf 1 can forward the resulting packet to either spine, at which point that switch matches the MPLS label 102, pops the label off the header, and forwards it to Leaf 2. Finally, Leaf 2 matches the destination IP address and forwards the packet along to Host 2.

What you should take away from this example is that SR is highly stylized. For a given combination of leaf and spine switches, Trellis first assigns all identifiers, with each rack configured to share an IP prefix and be on the same VLAN. Trellis then pre-computes the possible paths and installs the corresponding match/action rules in the underlying switches. The complexity having to do with balancing load across multiple paths is delegated to ECMP, which is similarly unaware of any end-to-end paths. From an implementation perspective, the Trellis control application that implements SR passes these match/action rules to ONOS, which in turn installs them on the underlying switches. Trellis also maintains its own Atomix map to manage the set of ECMP groups connecting leaf and spine switches.

7.3 Routes and Multicast

In addition to Segment Routing, which establishes data paths between leaf switches, Trellis also takes advantage of the Route and Mcast services introduced in Chapter 6. They determine which of the leaf-spine switches serve each IP prefix, and where to find all the hosts connected to each multicast group, respectively.

Trellis does not run distributed protocols like OSPF to learn about routes or PIM to construct multicast trees. Instead, it computes the right answers based on global information, and then pushes these mappings to the Route and Mcast services. This is straightforward to do because Trellis imposes the simplifying constraint that each rack corresponds to exactly one IP subnet.

```
onos> routes

B: Best route, R: Resolved route

Table: ipv4
B R  Network          Next Hop        Source (Node)
     0.0.0.0/0        172.16.0.1      FPM (127.0.0.1)
> *  1.1.0.0/18       10.0.1.20       STATIC
> *  10.0.99.0/24     10.0.1.1        FPM (127.0.0.1)
  *  10.0.99.0/24     10.0.6.1        FPM (127.0.0.1)
   Total: 2


Table: ipv6
B R  Network              Next Hop              Source (Node)
> *  2000::7700/120       fe80::288:ff:fe00:1   FPM (127.0.0.1)
> *  2000::8800/120       fe80::288:ff:fe00:2   FPM (127.0.0.1)
> *  2000::9900/120       fe80::288:ff:fe00:1   FPM (127.0.0.1)
  *  2000::9900/120       fe80::288:ff:fe00:2   FPM (127.0.0.1)
   Total: 3
```

Similarly, one can add a static route to the Route Service:

```
onos> route-add <prefix> <nexthop>
onos> route-add 1.1.0.0/18 10.0.1.20
onos> route-add 2020::101/120 2000::1
```

To make this discussion more concrete, consider that all the ONOS Services described in Chapter 6 can be invoked via a RESTful API, or alternatively, through a CLI that is a thin wrapper around REST's GET, POST and DELETE calls. Using the CLI to illustrate (because it is easier to read), one can query the Route service to learn the existing routes as shown in the example.

One thing to note about these examples is that there are two possible sources for routes. One is that the route is STATIC, which usually means that Trellis inserted it, with full knowledge of the what prefix it has assigned to each rack in the cluster. (Human operators could also add a STATIC route using the CLI, but this would be an exception rather than the rule.)

The second possibility is that FPM was the source. FPM (Forwarding Plane Manager) is yet another ONOS Service–one of the Trellis suite of services. Its job is to learn routes from external sources, which it does by tapping into a locally running Quagga process that is configured to peer with BGP neighbors. Whenever FPM learns about an external route, it adds the corresponding prefix-to-nexthop mapping to the Route service, indicating that the destination prefix is reachable via the leaf switches that connect the fabric to upstream networks (e.g., Switches 3 and 4 in Figure 37).

Multicast is similar. Again using the ONOS CLI, it is possible to create a new multicast route and add a sink to it. For example:

```
onos> mcast-host-join -sAddr *
    -gAddr 224.0.0.1
    -srcs 00:AA:00:00:00:01/None
    -srcs 00:AA:00:00:00:05/None
    -sinks 00:AA:00:00:00:03/None
    -sinks 00:CC:00:00:00:01/None
```

specifies *Any-Source Multicast (ASM)* (sAddr *), a multicast group address (gAddr), the group source addresses (srcs) and the group sink addresses (sinks). A sink can then be removed as follows:

```
onos> mcast-sink-delete -sAddr *
    -gAddr 224.0.0.1
    -h  00:AA:00:00:00:03/None
```

Again, there is no PIM running, but instead, Trellis offers a programmatic interface for network operators to define a multicast tree through a sequence of such calls. For example, when Trellis runs as part of an access network that delivers IPTV to subscribers, one option is for software running on the operator's set-top boxes to issue calls similar to the ones shown above (except, of course, using the RESTful API rather than the CLI). Another option is to have set-top boxes send IGMP messages, which Trellis intercepts using the Packet Service (similar to how the Host service intercepts ARP and DHCP packets). So the next time you use your TV remote to change channels, it is possible you are triggering procedure invocations up and down the SDN software stack described throughout this book!

7.4 Customized Forwarding

Trellis is an example use case for SDN. It is a set of control applications running top of a Network OS, which in turn runs on top of a collection of programmable switches arranged in a leaf-spine topology, where each switch runs a local Switch OS. In this way, Trellis serves as a capstone for our bottom-up tour of the SDN software stack.

But if we knew from the outset that a leaf-spine fabric supporting the Trellis feature-set was exactly what we wanted, we might go back to lower layers and tailor them for that purpose. This is what has happened over time with Trellis, resulting in a customized forwarding plane implemented by a P4 program called fabric.p4. We conclude this chapter by giving a high-level summary of fabric.p4, highlighting how its design meshes with the rest of the software stack.

Before doing that, it is important to acknowledge that knowing exactly what you want from a network at the outset is an impossibly high bar. Networks evolve based on experience using and operating them. No one knew how to write fabric.p4 on day one, but after iterating through a series of implementations of the other layers up-and-down the stack (including the introduction of Tofino as a programmable forwarding pipeline), fabric.p4 emerged. *The point is that treating the network as a programmable platform frees you to continually and rapidly evolve it.*

Said another way, we introduced forward.p4 as our canonical example of "a forwarding plane customized to do exactly what we want" in Chapter 4, but then spent the rest of the chapter describing all the machinery that makes something like forward.p4 possible, without ever revisiting what network-specific functionality it might actually implement. In short, fabric.p4 is a specific example of forward.p4, which we are only now able to describe because of how it relates to the control plane.

There are three things of note about fabric.p4. First, it is loosely based on the Broadcom OF-DPA pipeline, which makes sense because Trellis was originally implemented on top of a set of Tomahawk-based switches. The fabric.p4 pipeline is simpler than OF-DPA, as it eliminates tables that Trellis does not need. This makes fabric.p4 easier to control.

Second, fabric.p4 is designed to mimic ONOS's FlowObjective API, thereby simplifying the process of mapping FlowObjectives onto P4Runtime operations. This is best illustrated by Figure 39 which shows fabric.p4's ingress pipeline. The egress pipeline is not shown, but it is a straightforward rewriting of the header fields in the common case.

Third, fabric.p4 is designed to be configurable, making it possible to selectively include additional functionality. This is not easy when writing code that is optimized for an ASIC-based forwarding pipeline, and in practice it makes heavy use of pre-processor conditionals (i.e., #ifdefs). The code fragment shown below is the main control block of fabric.p4's ingress function. The details of the options are beyond to scope of this book, but at a high level:

- **SPGW (Serving and Packet Gateway):** Augments IP functionality in support of 4G Mobile Networks.

- **BNG (Broadband Network Gateway):** Augments IP functionality in support of Fiber-to-the-Home.

- **INT (Inband Network Telemetry):** Adds metric collection and telemetry output directives.

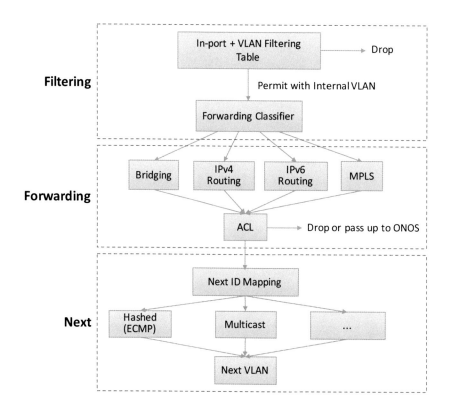

Figure 39: Logical pipeline supported by fabric.p4, designed to parallel the Filtering, Forwarding, and Next stages of the FlowObjective API.

For example, a companion file, spgw.p4 (not shown), implements the forwarding plane for the SPGW extension, which includes the GTP tunnel encapsulation/decapsulation required by the 3GPP cellular standard to connect the Trellis fabric to the base stations of the Radio Access Network. Similarly, bng.p4 (not shown) implements PPPoE termination, which is used by some Passive Optical Networks deployments to connect the Trellis fabric to home routers. Finally, it is worth nothing that the code fragment illustrates the basic structure of fabric.p4's core functionality, which first applies the *filtering objective* (filtering.apply), then applies the *forwarding objective* (forwarding.apply and acl.apply), and finally applies the *next objective* (next.apply).

```
apply {
#ifdef SPGW
    spgw_normalizer.apply(hdr.gtpu.isValid(), hdr.gtpu_ipv4,
        hdr.gtpu_udp, hdr.ipv4, hdr.udp, hdr.inner_ipv4,
        hdr.inner_udp);
#endif // SPGW

    // Filtering Objective
    pkt_io_ingress.apply(hdr, fabric_metadata, standard_metadata);
    filtering.apply(hdr, fabric_metadata, standard_metadata);
#ifdef SPGW
    spgw_ingress.apply(hdr.gtpu_ipv4, hdr.gtpu_udp, hdr.gtpu,
        hdr.ipv4, hdr.udp, fabric_metadata, standard_metadata);
#endif // SPGW

    // Forwarding Objective
    if (fabric_metadata.skip_forwarding == _FALSE) {
        forwarding.apply(hdr, fabric_metadata, standard_metadata);
    }
    acl.apply(hdr, fabric_metadata, standard_metadata);

    // Next Objective
    if (fabric_metadata.skip_next == _FALSE) {
        next.apply(hdr, fabric_metadata, standard_metadata);
#if defined INT
        process_set_source_sink.apply(hdr, fabric_metadata,
            standard_metadata);
#endif // INT
    }
#ifdef BNG
    bng_ingress.apply(hdr, fabric_metadata, standard_metadata);
#endif // BNG
}
```

VNF Off-loading

The SPGW and BNG extensions are examples of an optimization technique sometimes called VNF off-loading. VNF is an acronym for Virtual Network Function, which refers to functionality that sometimes runs as software in virtual machines. Off-loading refers to the idea of re-implementing this functionality to run in switch forwarding pipeline, rather than on a general-purpose server. This generally leads to better performance because packets can be forwarded from source to destination without having to be diverted to a server.

Calling out functions like SPGW and BNG as being an off-load "optimization" is arguably an example of selective memory. It's just as accurate to say that we've off-loaded IP to the switch since IP forwarding also sometimes runs in software on general-purpose processors. To a first approximation, SPGW and BNG are just specialized IP routers, augmented with additional features unique to cellular and wireline access networks, respectively. In the grand scheme of things, networks are built from a combination of forwarding functions, and we now have more options as to what hardware chip is the most appropriate target for implementing each such function.

In addition to selecting which extensions to include, the preprocessor also defines several constants, including the size of each logical table. Clearly, this implementation is a low-level approach to building configurable forwarding pipelines. Designing higher level language constructs for composition, including the ability to dynamically add functions to the pipeline at runtime, is a subject of on-going research.

Chapter 8: Future of SDN

It is still early days for SDN. Cloud-hosted control planes are being deployed in production networks, but we are only just starting to see SDN being trialed in access networks and programmable pipelines being used to introduce new data plane functionality. Enterprises have adopted network virtualization and SD-WAN to varying degrees, but there are still a lot more traditional networks than software-defined ones. As the technology matures and the APIs stabilize we expect to see increased adoption of the use cases discussed earlier, but it may be new use cases still on the horizon that have the biggest impact on the role SDN eventually plays. Indeed, the ability to support capabilities that were impossible in traditional networks is a great part of the promise of SDN. This chapter looks at two promising examples of emerging capabilities.

8.1 Verifiable Networks

Networks are notoriously difficult to make verifiably robust and secure against failures, attacks, and configuration mistakes. Despite progress on application-level security, little has been done to address the security and robustness of the underlying network infrastructure. And despite progress making computer networks more programmable, most networks are still built using closed/proprietary software and complex/fixed-function hardware, whose correctness is hard to prove and whose design has unknown provenance.

The emergence of 5G networks and applications will only exacerbate the situation. 5G networks will connect not only smart phones and people, but also everything from doorbells, to lights, refrigerators, self-driving cars, and drones. If we cannot secure these networks, the risk of cyber disasters is much worse than anything experienced to date.

A critical capability for securing the Internet is verifiability: the ability to ensure that every packet in the network follows an operator-specified path and encounters only a set of forwarding rules within every device that the operator intended. Nothing more and nothing less.

Experience has shown that verification works best in settings where the overall system is constructed in a compositional (i.e., disaggregated) manner. Being able to reason about small pieces makes verification tractable, and the reasoning needed to stitch the components together into the composite system can also lead to insights. With disaggregation as the foundation, verifiability follows from (a) the ability to state intent, and (b) the ability to observe behavior at fine granularity and in real-time. This is exactly the value SDN brings to the table, which leads to optimism that *verifiable closed-loop control* is now within reach.

Figure 40 illustrates the basic idea. The software stack described in this book is augmented with the measurement, code generation, and verification elements needed for verifiable closed-loop control. Fine-grained measurements can be implemented using INT (Inband Network Telemetry), which allows every packet to be stamped by the forwarding elements to indicate the path it took, the queueing delay it experienced, and the rules it matched. These measurements can then be analyzed and fed back into code generation and formal verification tools. This closed loop complements the intrinsic value of disaggregation, which makes it possible to reason about correctness-by-construction.

Further Reading:
N. Foster, et. al. Using Deep Programmability to Put Network Owners in Control. ACM SIGCOMM Computer Communication Review, October 2020.

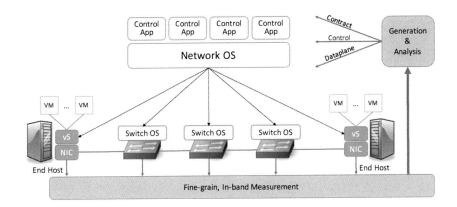

Figure 40: INT generates fine-grain measurements, which in turn feed a closed control loop that verifies the network's behavior.

The goal is to enable network operators to specify a network's behavior top-down, and then verifying the correctness across each interface. At the lowest level, P4 programs specify how packets are processed; these programs are compiled to run on the forwarding plane elements. Such an approach represents a fundamental new capability that has not been possible in conventional designs, based on two key insights.

Top-Down Verification

The approach to verifying networks described in this section is similar to the one used in chip design. At the top is a behavioral model; then at the register-transfer level is a Verilog or VHDL model; and eventually at the bottom are transistors, polygons and metal. Tools are used to formally verify correctness across each boundary and abstraction level.

This is a model for what we are talking about here: Verifying across boundaries in a top-down design approach. This is made possible by the new SDN interfaces and abstractions defined by the software stack, which extends all the way to the programmable forwarding pipelines provided by the switching chip.

As experience with hardware verification demonstrates, this approach works best in composed systems, where each minimal component can be verified or reliably tested on its own. Formal tools are then applied as components are composed at layer boundaries.

First, while network control planes are inherently complicated, a P4 data plane captures *ground truth* for the network—i.e., how it forwards packets—and is therefore an attractive platform for deploying verification technologies. By observing and then validating behavior at the data plane level, it is possible to reduce the trusted computing base: the switch operating system, driver, and other low-level components do not need to be trusted. Moreover, whereas the control plane tends to be written in a general-purpose language and is correspondingly complex, the data plane is necessarily simple: it is ultimately compiled to an efficient, feed-forward pipeline architecture with simple data types and limited state. While verifying general-purpose software is impossible in the general case, data plane verification is both powerful and practical.

This claim of practicality is grounded in the current state-of-the-art. Once the forwarding behavior is defined and known, then forwarding table state defines forwarding behavior. For example, if everything is known to be IPv4-forwarded, then the forwarding table state in all routers is enough to define the network behavior. This idea has been reduced to practice by techniques like Veriflow and Header Space Analysis (HSA), and is now available commercially. Knowing that this state is enough to verify networks with fixed forwarding behavior means that we are "merely" adding one new degree-of-freedom: allowing the network operator to program the forwarding behavior (and evolve it over time) using P4. The use of P4 to program the data plane is key: the language carefully excludes features such as loops and pointer-based data structures, which typically make analysis impractical. To read more about the opportunity, we recommend a paper by Jed Liu and colleagues.

The second insight is that, in addition to building tools for analyzing network programs, it is important to also develop technologies that provide higher levels of assurance through *defense-in-depth*. This addresses one of the main weaknesses of current approaches to network verification—they are based on mathematical models of the network components, and therefore can produce incorrect answers when those components behave in different ways than are captured in the model. By exploiting the ability of P4 data planes to collect rich

Further Reading:
J. Liu, et. al. p4v: Practical Verification for Programmable Data Planes. ACM SIGCOMM 2018.

telemetry and other monitoring data, it is possible to develop network verification tools that combine statically-verified components with runtime verification.

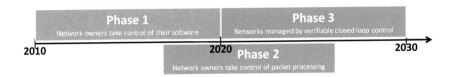

Figure 41: Projecting into the future, with Phase 3 of SDN focusing on verifiable, top-down control of network behavior.

To put this all in an historical context, Section 1.3 suggests we are now in the second phase of SDN. Figure 41 extends this into the future with a third phase, during which verifiable closed loop control will empower network operators to take full ownership of the software that defines their networks. This gives network owners further ability to tailor their networks in ways that differentiate them from their competitors.

8.2 SD-RAN

Much of the early hype surrounding 5G is about the increase in bandwidth it brings, but 5G's promise is mostly about the transition from a single access service (broadband connectivity) to a richer collection of edge services and devices, including support for immersive user interfaces (e.g., AR/VR), mission-critical applications (e.g., public safety, autonomous vehicles), and the Internet-of-Things (IoT). Many of these new applications will be feasible only if SDN principles are applied to the Radio Access Network (RAN), resulting in increased feature velocity. Because of this, mobile network operators are working to make Software-Defined RAN (SD-RAN) happen.

To understand SD-RAN at a technical level, it is important to recognize that the base stations that make up the RAN are, for all practical purposes, packet forwarders. The set of base stations in a given geographic area coordinate with each other to allocate the shared—and extremely scarce—radio spectrum. They make hand-off decisions, decide to jointly serve a given user (think of this as a RAN variant of link aggregation), and make packet scheduling decisions based on

Further Reading:
SD-RAN Project. Open Networking Foundation. August 2020.

the observed signal quality. Today these are purely local decisions, but transforming it into a global optimization problem is in SDN's wheelhouse.

The idea of SD-RAN is for each base station to report locally collected statistics about radio transmission quality back to a central SDN controller, which combines information from a set of base stations to construct a global view of how the radio spectrum is being utilized. A suite of control applications—for example, one focused on handoffs, one focused on link aggregation, one focused on load balancing, and one focused on frequency management—can then use this information to make globally optimal decisions, and push control instructions back to the individual base stations. These control instructions are not at the granularity of scheduling individual segments for transmission (i.e., there is still a real-time scheduler on each base station, just as an SDN-controlled ethernet switch still has a local packet scheduler), but they do exert near real-time control over the base stations, with control loops measured in less than ten milliseconds.

Like the verified closed-loop control example, the scenario just described is within reach, with a retargeting of ONOS at the SD-RAN use case already underway. Figure 42 shows the design, which introduces some new components, but largely builds on the existing ONOS architecture. In some cases, the changes are superficial. For example, ONOS adopts terminology coming out of the 3GPP and O-RAN standardization bodies,[18] most notably, that the NOS is called a *RAN Intelligent Controller (RIC)*. In other cases, it's a matter of adopting standardized interfaces: the **C1** interface by which control applications communicate with the RIC, the **A1** interface by which the operator configures the RAN, and the **E2** interface by which the RIC communicates with the underlying RAN elements. The details of these interfaces is beyond the scope of this book, but the important takeaway for our purposes is that they are no different than supporting any other standard north- or south-facing interface (e.g., gNMI, gNOI, OpenFlow).

[18] 3GPP (3rd Generation Partnership Project) has been responsible for standardizing the mobile cellular network ever since 3G, and O-RAN (Open-RAN Alliance) is a consortium of mobile network operators defining an SDN-based implementation strategy for 5G.

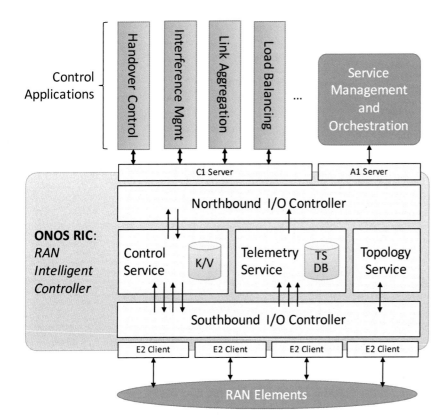

Figure 42: 3GPP-compliant RAN Intelligent Controller (RIC) built by adapting and extending ONOS.

The ONOS-based RIC takes advantage of the Topology Service described in Chapter 6, but it also introduces two new services: *Control* and *Telemetry*. The Control Service, which builds on the Atomix key/value store, manages the control state for all the base stations and user devices, including which base station is serving each user device, as well as the set of "potential links" that could connect the device. The Telemetry Service, which builds on a *Time Series Database (TSDB)*, tracks all the link quality information being reported back by the RAN elements. Various of the control applications then analyze this data to make informed decisions about how the RAN can best meet its data delivery objectives.

For a broad introduction into what's involved in disaggregating 5G mobile networks so they can be implemented in software, we recommend the following companion book.

Finally, circling back to the previous section, applying closed-loop verification to a disaggregated and software-defined cellular network is the next obvious thing to do.

Further Reading:
L. Peterson and O. Sunay. 5G Mobile Networks: A Systems Approach. June 2020.

Hands-on Programming

A collection of programming exercises provides hands-on experience with the software described in this book. They include:

- Using Stratum's P4Runtime, gNMI, OpenConfig, and gNOI interfaces

- Using ONOS to control P4-programmed switches

- Writing ONOS applications to implement control plane logic

- Testing a software stack using bmv2 in Mininet

- Using PTF to test P4-based forwarding planes

The exercises assume familiarity with Java and Python, although each exercise comes with starter code, so a high level of proficiency is not required. The exercises also use the *Mininet* network emulator, the *bmv2* P4-based switch emulator, the *PTF* Packet Testing Framework, and the *Wireshark* protocol analyzer. Additional information about each of these software tools is provided in the individual exercises.

The exercises originated with a *Next Generation SDN Tutorial* produced by ONF, and so they come with a collection of on-line tutorial slides that introduce the topics covered in the exercises:

- http://bit.ly/adv-ngsdn-tutorial-slides

These slides have significant overlap with the material covered in this book, so it is not essential that you start with the slides, but they can be a good supplemental resource.

Environment

You will be doing the exercises in a virtualized Linux environment running on your laptop. This section describes how to install and prepare that environment.

System Requirements

The current configuration of the VM is 4 GB of RAM and a 4-core CPU. These are the recommended minimum system requirements to complete the exercises. The VM also takes approximately 8 GB of HDD space. For a smooth experience, we recommend running the VM on a host system that has at least double these resources.

Download VM

Click the following link to download the VM (4 GB):

* http://bit.ly/ngsdn-tutorial-ova

The VM is in .ova format and has been created using VirtualBox v5.2.32. You can use any modern virtualization system to run the VM, although we recommend using VirtualBox. The following links provide instructions on how to get VirtualBox and import the VM:

* https://www.virtualbox.org/wiki/Downloads

* https://docs.oracle.com/cd/E26217_01/E26796/html/qs-import-vm.html

Alternatively, you can use these scripts to build a VM on your machine using Vagrant.

At this point you can start the virtual machine (an Ubuntu system), and log in using the credentials sdn / rocks. The instructions given throughout the remainder of this section (as well as the exercises themselves) are to be executed within the running VM.

Windows Users:
All scripts have been tested on MacOS and Ubuntu. Although they should work on Windows, they have not been tested. We therefore recommend that Windows users download the provided VM.

Clone Repository

To work on the exercises you will need to clone the following repo:

```
$ cd ~
$ git clone -b advanced \
  https://github.com/opennetworkinglab/ngsdn-tutorial
```

If the ngsdn-tutorial directory is already present in the VM, make sure to update its content:

```
$ cd ~/ngsdn-tutorial
$ git pull origin advanced
```

Note that there are multiple branches of the repo, each with a different configuration of the exercises. Always make sure you are in the advanced branch.

Upgrade Dependencies

The VM may have shipped with an older version of the dependencies than you need for the exercises. You can upgrade to the latest version using the following command:

```
$ cd ~/ngsdn-tutorial
$ make deps
```

This command downloads all necessary Docker images (~1.5 GB), which allows you to work through the exercises off-line.

Using an IDE

During the exercises you will need to write code in multiple languages (e.g., P4, Java, Python). While the exercises do not require the use of any specific IDE or code editor, one option is the Java IDE IntelliJ IDEA Community Edition, which comes pre-loaded with plugins for P4 syntax highlighting and Python development. We suggest using IntelliJ IDEA especially when working on the ONOS app, as it provides code completion for all ONOS APIs.

Repo Structure

The repo you cloned is structured as follows:

- p4src\ → Data Plane Implementation (P4)

- yang\ → Config Models (YANG)

- app\ → Custom ONOS app (Java)

- mininet\ → 2x2 leaf-spine (Mininet)

- util\ → Utility Scripts (Bash)

- ptf\ → Data plane unit tests (PTF)

Note that the exercises include links to various files on GitHub, but don't forget you have those same files cloned on your laptop.

Commands

To facilitate working on the exercises, the repo provides a set of make targets to control the different aspects of the process. The specific commands are introduced in the individual exercises, but the following is a quick reference:

- make deps → Pull and build all required dependencies

- make p4-build → Build P4 program

- make p4-test → Run PTF tests

- make start → Start Mininet and ONOS containers

- make stop → Stop all containers

- make restart → Restart containers clearing any previous state

- make onos-cli → Access the ONOS CLI (password: rocks, Ctrl-D to exit)

- make onos-log → Show the ONOS log

- make mn-cli → Access the Mininet CLI (Ctrl-D to exit)

- make mn-log $\rightarrow$ Show the Mininet log (i.e., the CLI output)

- make app-build $\rightarrow$ Build custom ONOS app

- make app-reload $\rightarrow$ Install and activate the ONOS app

- make netcfg $\rightarrow$ Push netcfg.json file (network config) to ONOS

Exercises

The following lists (and links) the individual exercises. That there are 8 exercises and 8 chapters is a coincidence. Exercises 1 and 2 focus on Stratum, and are best attempted after reading through Chapter 5. Exercises 3 through 6 focus on ONOS and are best attempted after reading through Chapter 6. Exercises 7 and 8 focus on Trellis and are best attempted after reading through Chapter 7. Note that the exercises build on each other, so it is best to work through them in order.

1. P4Runtime Basics

2. YANG, OpenConfig, gNMI Basics

3. Using ONOS as the Control Plane

4. Enabling ONOS Built-in Services

5. Implementing IPv6 Routing with ECMP

6. Implementing SRv6

7. Trellis Basics

8. GTP Termination with fabric.p4

You can find solutions for each exercise in the solution subdirectory for the repo you cloned. Feel free to compare your solution to the reference solution should you get stuck.

If you have suggestions for how we can improve these exercises, please send email to ng-sdn-exercises@opennetworking.org or post an issue to https://github.com/opennetworkinglab/ngsdn-tutorial/issues/new on GitHub.

Executing Commands:
As a reminder, these commands will be executed in a terminal window you open within the VM you just created. Be sure you are in the root directory of the repo you cloned (where the main Makefile lives).

Graphical Interfaces:
When exercises call for viewing graphical output, you will see reference to the *ONF Cloud Tutorial Portal*. This is for cloud-hosted VMs used during ONF-run tutorials, and so does apply here. In its place, the exercises also describe how to access the GUI running locally on your laptop.

About The Book

Source for *Software-Defined Networks: A Systems Approach* is available on GitHub under terms of the Creative Commons (CC BY-NC-ND 4.0) license. The community is invited to contribute corrections, improvements, updates, and new material under the same terms. If you make use of this work, the attribution should include the following information:

> *Title: Software-Defined Networks: A Systems Approach*
> *Authors: Larry Peterson, Carmelo Cascone, Brian O'Connor,*
> *Thomas Vachuska, and Bruce Davie*
> *Source:* https://github.com/SystemsApproach/SDN
> *License:* CC BY-NC-ND 4.0

Read the Book

This book is part of the Systems Approach Series, with an online version published at https://sdn.systemsapproach.org.

To track progress and receive notices about new versions, you can follow the project on Facebook and Twitter. To read a running commentary on how the Internet is evolving, follow the Systems Approach Blog.

Build the Book

To build a web-viewable version, you first need to download the source:

```
$ mkdir ~/SDN
$ cd ~/SDN
$ git clone https://github.com/SystemsApproach/SDN.git
```

The build process is stored in the Makefile and requires Python
be installed. The Makefile will create a virtualenv (doc_venv) which
installs the documentation generation toolset. To generate HTML in
_build/html, run

```
$ make html
```

Contribute to the Book

We hope that if you use this material, you are also willing to contribute back to it. If you are new to open source, you might check out
this How to Contribute to Open Source guide. Among other things,
you'll learn about posting *Issues* that you'd like to see addressed, and
issuing *Pull Requests* to merge your improvements back into GitHub.

About The Authors

Larry Peterson is the Robert E. Kahn Professor of Computer Science, Emeritus at Princeton University, where he served as Chair from 2003-2009. His research focuses on the design, implementation, and operation of Internet-scale distributed systems, including the widely used PlanetLab and MeasurementLab platforms. He is currently leading the CORD and Aether access-edge cloud projects at the Open Networking Foundation (ONF), where he serves as CTO. Peterson is a member of the National Academy of Engineering, a Fellow of the ACM and the IEEE, the 2010 recipient of the IEEE Kobayashi Computer and Communication Award, and the 2013 recipient of the ACM SIGCOMM Award. He received his Ph.D. degree from Purdue University in 1985.

Carmelo Cascone is a Member of the Technical Staff at the Open Networking Foundation (ONF), where he currently leads technical activities around the adoption of programmable switches, P4, and P4Runtime in ONF projects such as ONOS, CORD, and Aether. Cascone received a Ph.D. from Politecnico di Milano in 2017, in a joint program with École Polytechnique de Montréal. He is broadly interested in computer networks and systems, with a focus on data plane programmability and Software-Defined Networking (SDN).

Brian O'Connor is a Member of the Technical Staff at the Open Networking Foundation (ONF), where he currently leads technical activities around the adoption of switch operating systems. O'Connor received a BS and MS in Computer Science from Stanford Univesity in 2012 and 2013, respectively.

Thomas Vachuska is Chief Architect at the Open Networking Foundation (ONF), where he leads the ONOS project. Before joining ONF, Vachuska was a Software Architect at Hewlett-Packard. Vachuska received a BA in Mathematics from California State University-Sacramento in 1994.

Bruce Davie is a computer scientist noted for his contributions to the field of networking. He is a former VP and CTO for the Asia Pacific region at VMware. He joined VMware during the acquisition of Software Defined Networking (SDN) startup Nicira. Prior to that, he was a Fellow at Cisco Systems, leading a team of architects responsible for Multiprotocol Label Switching (MPLS). Davie has over 30 years of networking industry experience and has co-authored 17 RFCs. He was recognized as an ACM Fellow in 2009 and chaired ACM SIGCOMM from 2009 to 2013. He was also a visiting lecturer at the Massachusetts Institute of Technology for five years. Davie is the author of multiple books and the holder of more than 40 U.S. Patents.

Made in the USA
Monee, IL
20 October 2021